In *It'll be Okay* Sheryl Giesbrecht Turner gives hope, help, and healing for the doubting, hurting, questioning, or confused soul. Sheryl is an overcoming woman who has been through many life trials and tribulations. In taking her own questions to God, she helps us find answers for our own.
—Pam Farrel, author of 45 books including *Discovering Hope in the Psalms:A Creative Bible Study Experience* and *7 Simple Skills for Every Woman: Success in Keeping It All Together*

If "doubting God" is your guilty secret, reading *It'll Be Okay* will slay the guilt as you discover how God wants to use your doubt as a pathway to deeper faith.
—Connie Cavanaugh, speaker and author of *From Faking It to Finding Grace: Discovering God Again When Your Faith Runs Dry* www.conniecavanaugh.com

I love that Sheryl assures us that we can embrace our doubts and let them be a catalyst for finding deeper faith. Asking hard questions is not a sin. Rather, it is the way to understanding. Left-brained, logic-loving person that I am, I embrace God's invitation: "Come, let us reason together."
—Jennifer Kennedy Dean, author of Live a Praying Life® publications; executive director of The Praying Life Foundation

i

Doubt. That shameful word that implies we're not smart enough or don't have enough faith. Sheryl Giesbrecht Turner in her latest book, *It'll Be Okay*, tackles doubt to help readers increase their vision toward good and fulfilling life solutions. In fact, Sheryl bravely tells us that by addressing doubt, we will increase our confidence and grow in our faith. In a beautiful rhythm of research, biblical truths, and Sheryl's raw and personal stories, this captivating and well-written book will inspire you to allow God to redefine your life from doubt to "It'll be Okay."

—Heidi McLaughlin, international speaker and author of *Restless for More, Sand to Pearls* and *Beauty Unleashed* www. heartconnection.ca

In *It'll Be Okay*, Sheryl shares her own deeply personal experiences with doubt—from her battle with cancer to the shame of past drug abuse. She examines the many ways doubt affects our emotions, our peace, and our relationship with God. Through the use of reflective stories and empowering scriptures, Sheryl offers hope for those times when there appear to be no satisfactory answers. This book is a fresh drink of Living Water for the spiritually thirsty.

—Dr. Saundra Dalton-Smith, award-winning author of *Come Empty: Pour Out Life's Hurts and Receive God's Healing Love* and *Sacred Rest: Recover Your Life, Renew Your Energy, Restore Your Sanity*

With compelling candor, Giesbrecht Turner releases the grip of doubt on the human soul. Through raw storytelling, clear application of biblical truth, and gentle encouragement, Giesbrecht Turner takes you from a place of doubt, despair, and darkness, cracking open just enough truth to flood you with light. If you are struggling with God, your past, or your current relationships, this book is exactly the hope and practical help you need!

—Erica Wiggenhorn, Bible teacher and author of *An Unexplainable Life: Recovering the Joy and Wonder of the Early Church*

When life leaves you with more questions than answers, this book is your guide to discovering peace, purpose, and your true identity.

—Monica Schmelter, TV host of Bridges; General Manager, WHTN Christian Television Network; speaker and author

If we are honest with ourselves, we all walk through rooms full of doubt in dark times. *It'll Be Okay* reminds us of God's irresistible love bringing us hope during discouragement and light for passing through the shadows of life. A book full of strength and courage for our journey.

—Jean Wise, author, speaker, and spiritual director

Sheryl Giesbrecht Turner has taken her brokenness and sorrow and turned it into an empowering message. The concept of doubt being a positive thing, as it pushes you toward God instead of away from him, is vital for us to embrace. The enemy wants to use doubts to destroy our faith, but God allows them to strengthen us in him. A chilling deathblow to the enemy's kingdom, *It'll Be Okay: Finding God When Doubt Hides the Truth*, illuminates the significance of working through our doubts and coming out the other end victorious. Highly recommended!

—Athena Dean Holtz
Speaker, publisher, former radio host and pastor's wife
Redemption Press: Where Your Message Is Our Mission
Proud sponsor of the 2018 WOMEN OF JOY tour, *Rescued*
www.redemption-press.com

Do you wonder where God is when you need him? Do you question if he loves you and if he will take care of you? If you answered yes to any of these questions, *It'll Be Okay:Finding God When Doubt Hides the Truth* is the book for you.

Sheryl Giesbrecht Turner offers you comfort, compassion, and hope. Her tender approach and transparency will help you understand you are not alone. You will find your identity in Christ, not in the lies of the enemy, and thus experience peace and freedom.

Sheryl carefully weaves in Bible verses and shows us from the lives of people in the Bible and from her own life what a mighty God we serve, who fights our battles for us. I highly recommend this book to pastors, chaplains, counselors, and church librarians. Buy a copy for yourself and one for a friend too.

—Yvonne Ortega, Licensed Professional Counselor, Licensed Substance Abuse Treatment Practitioner, Clinically Certified Domestic Violence Counselor
Moving from Broken to Beautiful® through Grief

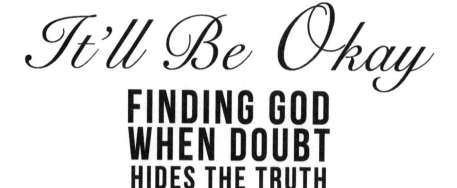

It'll Be Okay

FINDING GOD
WHEN DOUBT
HIDES THE TRUTH

Sofi –
so excited to hear your thoughts!

It'll Be Okay

FINDING GOD
WHEN DOUBT
HIDES THE TRUTH

Rom 12:2

Sheryl Giesbrecht Turner

SHERYL GIESBRECHT TURNER
foreword by **DON PIPER**

REDEMPTION
P R E S S

Published by Redemption Press, PO Box 427, Enumclaw, WA 98022

Toll Free (844) 2REDEEM (273-3336)

Redemption Press is honored to present this title in partnership with the author. The views expressed or implied in this work are those of the author. Redemption Press provides our imprint seal representing design excellence, creative content, and high quality production.

Unless otherwise noted, all Scriptures are taken from the Holy Bible, New International Version®, NIV®. Copyright © 1973, 1978, 1984, 2011 by Biblica, Inc.™ Used by permission of Zondervan. All rights reserved worldwide. www.zondervan.com

Neil Anderson, *Victory Over the Darkness*. Copyright © 2000 Bethany House, a division of Baker Publishing Group. Used by permission.

ISBN: 978-1-68314-572-1 (Paperback)
978-1-68314-573-8 (ePub)
978-1-68314-574-5 (Mobi)

Library of Congress Catalog Card Number: 2018930273

FOREWORD

You're about to read an important book, in my opinion. *It'll Be Okay: Finding God When Doubt Hides the Truth* is an enormously caring and relevant book written by someone who personally understands her subject.

Sheryl Giesbrecht Turner has endured what Mother Theresa calls "the dark night of the soul." And while the process of emerging into the light remains challenging and often ongoing, praise God, there is light.

Yes, there is hope even in the midst of abject doubt. So many feel trapped in the midst of what Giesbrecht Turner calls "a gloomy motionless tunnel" or "situations that keep you up all night." The author examines the universal dilemma of doubt that all too frequently plagues us all. And she boldly and with deep, personal transparency tackles the question: Can faith really overcome doubt?

In an era when the institution of the nuclear family and certainly fatherhood are being challenged, Giesbrecht Turner explores the critical issue of "spiritual fatherlessness." She provides great insight into the quintessential "doubter," Thomas, and the supreme "sufferer," Job. And she does it with compassion, humor, clarity, and happily... real application. Indeed, her goal is quite simply to help us "roll back the fog of doubt." And she endeavors to help us understand that God sometimes allows suffering to come for reasons only God understands.

Her consistent use of biblical insight and her own experiences as a cancer survivor, an abuse survivor while a youth, and a widow, offer us tremendous opportunity for personal growth and victory over doubt and suffering. We certainly will not be able to grow while still holding on to "yesterday's junk."

It's my conviction that one of the most beneficial aspects of *It'll Be Okay: Finding God When Doubt Hides the Truth* is the author's inclusion of a "Who I am is who I am in Christ" list of Bible promises. These assurances are exciting and ultimately encouraging to all who seek to overcome the slings and arrows of this life.

But overcoming is a choice. Until the curtain rings down on this fragile planet, it will always be a choice.

And now you've chosen to read an important book about overcoming. Bring your sorrows and doubts to the table. When you read the final page of this tome I pray that your faith will be fortified. Sheryl Giesbrecht Turner wisely counsels, "faith prevails." Her sincere desire for you is "to introduce you to the one who can answer your questions and give you hope to solve the situations that keep you up at night."

Now, that IS important!

—Don Piper
Pastor and *New York Times* Bestselling Author
90 Minutes in Heaven: A True Story of Death and Life
Fleming Revell/Baker
Heaven Is Real: Lessons On Earthly Joy
Daily Devotionals: 90 Readings for Hope and Healing
Getting to Heaven: Instructions On How to Live Now
Random House/Penguin/Berkley

INTRODUCTION

For six months, I wondered why God was holding out on me. I prayed. There was silence. I thought it might help if I prayed harder and longer. I was wrong. My unanswered prayers seemed to bounce off the ceiling; my requests appeared overlooked. It felt as if God were playing hide-and-seek. I needed answers, direction, and wisdom, and it didn't look as though any were approaching. I'd grown accustomed to walking in the welcome light of peace and reason, but now God's illumination was shrouded by despair. I wondered, *Did God want to be found?* A thick fog of depression clouded my view of a heavenly Being. The relationship I had formerly experienced with him, once comfortable and close, now felt awkward, dutiful, and cold.

Ever lost your way? Of course, most of us have ended up at a destination different from the one at which we'd intended to arrive. One time I diligently followed handwritten instructions to a friend's home. Although I meticulously followed those directions, I did not know at the time that there was one street name missing. I had to guess where to find the correct turnoff, and when I guessed incorrectly I ended up in a place I hadn't planned to be. I later learned I'd traveled in the exact opposite direction from my destination! At one time or another while driving, we each find ourselves off course and need to find an accurate map, up-to-date directions, or a dependable GPS. At times the courses our lives take might feel the same way—we become confused, lost, or even as if we are going backward. We need clear direction, and it's hard when that direction doesn't seem forthcoming.

In a season like that, I wasn't sure I could count on God. I doubted God would come through for me because I didn't sense his guidance. I believed in God, but I didn't know there was a difference between believing God and believing *in* God to provide what I needed. I kept telling myself, "It'll be okay." Yet somehow I wasn't sure "it" would be okay. I'd been trying to serve God and live for Him for a few years. I was a graduate of a Bible college. I'd led prayer groups and Bible studies for teenage girls, and I was married to a pastor. I knew how to believe God for other people. My faith was put to the test when I would pray for others, and God would come through. It seemed he was there to work out things for other people. I wasn't convinced God would do the same for me. I wondered, *God, what about me?* I began to doubt God.

I was in a very dark place physically, emotionally, and spiritually. Some attributed my issues to a physical need—was I taking care of my body? Was I getting enough sleep? Or even worse, did I have an undiagnosed medical or emotional condition? Some chalked up my concerns as a choice to carry emotional baggage. I didn't agree with any of those diagnoses.

Frequent flyers know what it is like to trust an airplane pilot to land a plane in zero visibility. To me, that's what it is like to trust God when you can't "see, hear, or feel" him. Pilots trust their radar and depend on their landing gear, and likewise, we must learn how to trust God's heart when we can't see his hand. At the time, I didn't know how much more to my walk with him I had yet to experience, learned only by walking though the zero visibility of the fog of doubt.

Doubts need to be addressed, or they will rot your faith from the inside out. Be honest with God and yourself. Dealing with doubt to the point of renewed belief brings spiritual strength. Don't be afraid to doubt. The Bible would not be relevant to real life struggles and joyful discoveries without the intriguing and notable accounts of the "doubters." Remember Abraham, Zechariah, Thomas, Gideon, Jonah, Naomi, and John the Baptist?

Don't be afraid to seek answers. God is not threatened by our questions, logic, science, or emotions. Along with our fallible humanity, we must be able to grasp the existence of a loving, omniscient, omnipresent, infinite, and everlasting good God. As you read, I hope your faith will be renewed. I pray your spirit will be revived. My desire is for you to be refreshed in your view of God as he shows you how to push away the fog of doubt and let the light of truth shine through. Let's go deeper together, seeking his face and receiving a faith that is a foundation able to withstand any storm.

"I do believe; help me overcome my unbelief!"
Mark 9:24

"Blessed is she who has believed that the Lord would fulfill his promises to her!"
Luke 1:45

"Doubt can be a tool in God's hand wielded, in the lives of those who allow it, for the strengthening, not the destruction of faith."
George MacDonald
Scottish author, poet, and minister 1824–1905

TABLE OF CONTENTS

Chapter 1:

PAT ANSWERS

"Only the one who knows nothing doubts nothing."
French proverb

Sixty-six years of letters. Through this trove of handwritten correspondence to her confidantes and superiors, this godly woman shared her thoughts, concerns, losses, disappointments, and doubts. Over the course of six decades' worth of honest revelations in her heartfelt confessions, she bared her wounded soul to those she trusted. Writing the letters offered a safe place for her to express her hopes—and her doubts.

And then she ordered them to be destroyed once they were received and read.

"Jesus has a very special love for you," the desperate woman wrote in one of the remaining correspondences. "But as for me, the silence and emptiness is so great, that I look and do not see. Listen and do not hear—the tongue moves (in prayer) but does not speak…I want you to pray for me—that I let him have a free hand." Mother Teresa

Mother Teresa? The same Mother Teresa who won a Nobel Peace Prize for her work with the lepers and the poor? She also doubted God? The naked reality of her raw words is almost a contradiction; it exposed the truth of how she really felt. Her obvious disconnect between what she knew of God and what she felt from him was vulnerably characterized as her "dark night of the soul"; she was encased in a spiritual murkiness. She revealed the feeble truth: for fifty years of her life, she'd felt no presence of God whatsoever—either in "her heart or the Eucharist." It's probable the distance she felt from God began at about the same time she began caring for the dying leprous colonies in Calcutta. Although Mother Teresa pulled things together in public and for those she served, in the more than forty communications, this saint grieved over her private and personal "dryness, darkness, loneliness, and torture." She compared her existence to hell and at one point said it had driven her to doubt the existence of heaven and even of God. Acutely aware of the discrepancy between her inner state and her public demeanor, she said, "The smile is a mask or a cloak that covers everything."[1] And no one, except God and her confessors, knew of her torment. I don't know about you, but I can certainly relate.

Longing for answers

"Where is God? Is he there? Does he care?" Maybe you too have yearned for the presence of God, and he seemed distant. Your situation may not be as severe as Mother Teresa's, but you feel abandoned and desolate. When we are in the middle of a gloomy, emotionless tunnel, "Where is God?" is the query we ask our creator as we beg him to stop the pain. It's hard to doubt our doubts, that is, to question them to see if they are really what they appear to be in light of our faith, because they seem very real to us. We, like Mother Teresa, wonder if we can make sense of suffering. In a recent Facebook survey, I asked, "What is the one question that keeps you up at night?" The responses varied from examining doubt to pondering concerns about one's future or the status of a deceased loved one. Here is a sample of those responses:

"Why are we told that God has the perfect spouse in store for our lives in his perfect timing, and yet we aren't even guaranteed tomorrow to be alive?"

"Retirement, health, money…Lord, you promise to care for your saints into old age what does that mean?"

"Am I doing a good job as a mother?"

"Where is my biological father?"

"When my husband leaves for the week for work, I wonder and ask God if my husband remains faithful to me. My rough past makes the future tough when it is time to trust. But do I really want to know?"

"Is tragedy (a baby's death, a person killed by a drunk driver) part of God's plan and we don't see the big picture? Or does it occur because we live in a sin-filled world where stuff happens, and God doesn't stop the tragedies but grieves with us in them?"

"Is my late boyfriend in heaven? We talked and I prayed, but I don't know for sure."

"How can we overlook the refugees?"

"Why does God give and then take away?"

"How will Christians survive what's coming—how can we prepare?"

Can you relate to those heartfelt pleas? I certainly can. People of faith, like them, like us, can doubt God's goodness, his love, his plan, his attentiveness. Perhaps your concerns are not listed here, but let me assure you, whatever they are, God cares. Together, we will search the scriptures and seek an answer to this heartfelt plea: Can faith really win over doubt in the multiple miserable circumstances we all must undergo? What is our role? What is God's role? Throughout this book, we will discover how faith prevails.

Fully alive

We must begin by building upon the premise of God's love for us. God created us for one original purpose: union with him. Did you know we were on God's mind from the beginning of time? "Long before he laid down the earth's foundations, he had us in mind" (Ephesians 1:4, MSG). We are created with a core need to feel fully alive. God created us with the requirement that to feel fully alive, we need to experience his unconditional love, acceptance, and security. As God is the only one who can meet this need, we need him to live our best life.

Before we are aware of the love of God, we are in the dark about his plans for us. Somewhere deep inside of us is a longing to be earnestly searched for and found by somebody wonderful. We may try to deny it. Outrun it. Numb it. We may try to keep this longing hidden or attempt to keep it wrapped up. But when we least expect it, this yearning will surface. We hunger to be unconditionally treasured and unreservedly prized. This intense longing to be deeply loved and cherished is embedded in our nature. God made us with a profound need, a necessity to be loved by him.

The answer

I am the firstborn of four children. My dad always called me "Princess" because I was the apple of his eye. I remember when he taught me how to ride a bike. He removed the training wheels on my Schwinn and, giving me a running shove, said, "Be careful, sweetie." His strong voice cautioned me to avoid an object in the road. I was seated securely on the banana seat, both hands on the handlebars, and as I rolled forward, the front tire still wobbled. Yet the sound of his voice gave me the confidence I needed to move ahead despite my lack of experience. I focused intently on the path ahead and replied, "Yes, Father."

Maybe you cannot relate to God as a caring, tender, and involved father such as this. You might have been disappointed by your dad, one who did not speak encouraging words or look out for you. If not you, then certainly people you know have felt dismissed or overlooked by their own fathers. Inattentive, uncaring, or absent fathers make up an epidemic proportion of fathers in America. According to a recent study, "15 million American children—one in three—live without a father present in their homes. Many of these children are physically, emotionally, or sexually abused by their mothers, fathers, or parents' live-in partner. These factors result in less-than-average academic achievement, and higher-than-average teenage pregnancy, drug use, and crime."[2] America's social problems take into consideration the absence of fathers in our homes. This fatherlessness affects us on a spiritual level too.

Well then, we might ask, why don't I feel loved by God?

"Spiritual fatherlessness" causes a disconnection, a breach between the natural father and our spiritual heavenly father. Many of us don't have a good relationship, or any relationship, with our earthly fathers (becoming effectively fatherless), and therefore we don't with our heavenly father either. The latter condition is called "spiritual fatherlessness." The devil sets out to destroy harmony in our most valued relationships. This isn't necessarily a physical breach; it can often be a spiritual battle, with the devil using those who mean the most to us to keep us from God. This is why many, myself included, struggled with whether we believe in God. Our ability to believe in a good, present, and attentive heavenly father might be hampered by our feeling of disconnectedness through "spiritual fatherlessness"[3] brought on by difficulties in what were once loving, earthly relationships.

During my junior high years, Dad and I exchanged harsh words, disagreed violently, and regularly engaged in shouting matches with each other. I thought I knew what was best for my life and was determined to show my father and the rest of my family I was better off without everyone telling me what to do. Unfortunately, I was clueless about the enemy's tactics to divide our family. I was rebellious and proud, and could not respond to my father's attempts to show me love. I was listening to the wrong voices, not my earthly nor my heavenly father's.

At seventeen, I careened deep into drug addiction. I stayed high and distracted as often as possible, trying to fill the emptiness in my life with the highest high or the cutest guy. No matter what I did, though, my need for affection only increased. I couldn't wait to move out of my parents' home. My family would step in to help whether I wanted them to or not—they even pulled strings to get me a volunteer summer job at a Christian camp. It was an opportunity to get out of the house, so I took it. Once I was there, the camp staff assigned me lists of chores, which included washing hundreds of dishes in the mess hall, raking piles of pine needles around the campgrounds, and even moving logs around the outdoor campfire ring.

I didn't enjoy these tasks, of course. Whenever I complained or threw fits over doing my chores, or smoked cigarettes and dope, the camp staff responded with kindness, affection, and love. "Love covers a multitude of sins," they repeated to me over and over, immersing me in their, and God's, unconditional love during my two week stay. The words rang in my ears; I couldn't get the six-word saying off my mind. I found out later that the sentence they quoted was a Bible verse: 1 Peter 4:8. Soon after camp, I discovered that the Bible was not just another book, but the inspired word of God. The Bible is a road map to help us find God's rules by which to live, as well as better understand his love, the motivation to live his way. I began to see the results of God's word exhibited in the lives of the people who worked at the camp. The staff didn't tell me to change anything about my appearance, attitude, or addictions. Instead, they showed me what the invitation of love looked like. They were kind; they offered the true love of God without forcing me to accept it.

After two weeks of experiencing how love covered a multitude of my sins, I embraced the other camp staffers' love—and God's. In the years before coming to the camp, I questioned God's love because I looked at people who loved me inconsistently or according to their standards, not God's. I'd expected to be accepted as I was, but in my church youth group I was told not to wear my black nail polish, spiked hair, or flowing capes. I wanted badly to fit in, yet at home, school, and even church, people told me I didn't belong because my looks, attitudes, and habits were different from theirs. The camp staff's generous daily offerings of God's word made me aware of God's love through their voices and actions. They accepted and included me just the way I was, seeing my insides, and not merely what I presented on the outside. For the first time in my life, I felt I was in the right place, completely accepted and needed.

The night my hardened heart melted to accept the irresistible love of God was a defining moment. I didn't have to clean up my act. Jesus's death, his precious blood, had paid for my sins, and realizing that fact enabled me to trust him to do that for me. Because of his resurrection, all I had to do was approach and communicate with God, my perfect heavenly father. I finally understood the disruption in my relationship with God—we'd been disconnected through my sin and my cloudy vision of what God was like—and my relationship with my spiritual father was restored through the sacrifice of his son. It radically changed my life, and I want that for you too.

The purpose of this book is to introduce you to the one who can answer your questions: God. And to give you hope to address the situations that keep you up at night. You read about my camp encounter with God. He gave me and has given each of us a choice—to follow him or not. Remember, we are created by God for a relationship with God and will only feel our best when that relationship is established and real. Former atheist C. S. Lewis says, "God made us: invented us as a man invents an engine. A car is made to run on petrol, and it would not run properly on anything else. Now God designed the human machine to run on Himself. He Himself is the fuel our spirits were designed to burn, or the food our spirits were designed to feed on. There is no other."[4]

Believe it or not

I had been a doubter for a few years before I was sent off to the summer camp. But after several days immersed in the kind, inclusive, and loving ways of the camp staff, I began to believe God's love could cover the things that held me captive: drugs and alcohol, lying and stealing, promiscuity and drug dealing. It was finally clear. I didn't need to clean up my act before coming to God; he loved me passionately just the way I was. God adopted me into his family. "God decided in advance to adopt us into his own family by bringing us to himself through Jesus Christ. This is what he wanted to do, and it gave him great pleasure" (Ephesians 1:5, NLT).

Gently, tenderly, he guided me and took away the spiritual blindfold I thought would protect me from life's pain, and yet, when he removed it, he helped me face my longing to be loved, and then he fulfilled that longing. With my heavenly father's protection and presence, I received healing for my human "father wound". I could accept God's forgiveness from my guilt once and for all. That was the beginning of my spiritual journey, and it was a wonderful beginning. Soon after that, though, I would take my next step on my faith path: overcoming doubt.

The most famous doubter

After His resurrection, Jesus appeared to all the disciples except Thomas. We don't know why Thomas was absent when Jesus presented himself to the disciples. Yet even when the other disciples told him, "We have seen the Lord!" (John 20:23), Thomas refused to believe that Christ had risen from the dead. "But he said to them, 'Unless I see the nail marks in his hands and put my finger where the nails were, and put my hand into his side, I will not believe it' " (John 20:25).

Thomas has been given a bad rap over the generations; he was a doubter with a purpose—he wanted to know the truth. He didn't idolize his doubts; he was a glad believer when he was given reasons to be. He explained his doubts. He didn't try to get others to side with him, but he wanted proof. Living proof. Most of us can identify with that, can't we? Doubting was not Thomas's way of life—it was his way of responding to life's uncertainties. Doubt like Thomas's can be a positive thing, especially if it brings us closer to God. Doubt can help shape our faith, as you will hear in the following chapters.

After my conversion to Christ at age seventeen, I walked with the Lord without question for several years. However, as God began to show me his plans for my faith to grow and for me to more deeply trust him, I struggled with doubt and was offered the opportunity to press through those doubts and believe God more. Have you ever pushed through to a new level of spiritual growth, only to be challenged again to go deeper and farther?

Defining moment

It's interesting to consider that "doubt" comes from the Greek word *distazo*—from *dis* meaning "twice" or "double." Doubt happens when we double-think a concept or an idea, or re-entertain a thought. It's something like second thoughts. Further, the word "dubious" comes from Latin *duitare* or *dubius* from which we get "dubious"—questionable.

One of the most important things to understand is that there are two different aspects of doubt:

1. Unbelief, disbelief, rejection, denial, agnosticism, faithlessness.
2. Uncertainty, lack of confidence, reservation, problematic, misgivings, skeptical, questioning, wavering, indeterminate.[5]

Once we explore the difference, I hope you'll be free from the guilt, shame, or fear that can sometimes accompany recognizing our doubts.

The first aspect of doubt is unbelief. For believers, unbelief happens when we choose to turn away from God, often during times of great emotional, physical, or spiritual distress. Doubts inevitably trickle in, bringing us to examine God and our faith in him. Unbelief causes us to turn our backs on God, because we don't believe he is coming through for us the way we think he should. In contrast, unbelievers like Pharaoh exhibited unbelief by rejecting God altogether, as shown in Exodus 9:12: "But the LORD hardened Pharaoh's heart and he would not listen to Moses and Aaron, just as the LORD had said to Moses." It is important to understand that God did not intentionally harden Pharaoh's heart and overrule his free will. No, God simply confirmed Pharaoh free choice to live a life of refusing to submit to God. In the same way, after a lifetime of resisting God, you might find you have no desire to turn to him; your heart may be hardened too. Please turn to God now while you have a chance. If you continue to ignore God's voice, someday you won't be able to hear it at all. There is a "Love Letter to My Readers" in the back of this book that shows you how to respond to God, giving your heart to him rather than allowing it to be hardened by unbelief.

Doubt for certainty

Uncertainty is the second aspect of doubt. Uncertainty recognizes doubt and then takes time to examine it with the ultimate goal of finding the fine line between unbelief (no faith) and uncertainty (faith when all the answers aren't immediately forthcoming). Faith can be a process bringing us to examine our beliefs and, as Thomas experienced, to question

God: "Show me proof" or "Why me?" We need to let the tension between doubt and belief become faith-producing as we tell God all about our doubts. Uncertainty actually builds faith when the quest for certainty meets with success. This was the case for Thomas in his discussion with Jesus. Jesus's reply? "Then he said to Thomas, 'Put your finger here; see my hands. Reach out your hand and put it into my side. Stop doubting and believe.' Thomas said to him, 'My Lord and my God!' " (John 20:27-28). Author John Ortberg frames the concept like this: "Will you keep going when you don't know why? When you can't get any answers that would make the pain go away, will you still say, 'My Lord,' even though his ways are not clear to you? Will you keep going—with all the grace and grit and faith you can muster—and live in hope that one day God will set everything right?"[6]

Doubt becomes belief

I wasted my teenage years as I searched for meaning, purpose, and identity in things and people who could never fill my God-shaped void. In my case, this gaping "father wound" was not caused by "fatherlessness" but by my own selfishness, though that will not be the case for everyone. Thankfully, I learned to turn from my earthly plans and still want my heavenly father's will more than my own. God graciously showed me how to release every disappointment that I had imagined or feared and to put my trust in him. I felt used by those I thought were my friends, even though we didn't have much in common except our priority to stay high and party as much as possible. Being loved and accepted by a perfect heavenly father gave me a new high, faithful friends, and spiritual stability as I found freedom from my addictions and codependent behaviors.

This step towards freedom takes trust and transparency. If you don't view God as someone you can trust, maybe your view has become blocked by hurts, habits, or hang-ups. God wants to heal your "father wound". He wants you to ask for his help.

With my renewed understanding of the place of the heavenly Father's love relationship in my life and of Thomas's certain belief, I was able to move beyond my doubt. Once we allow God to heal our "father wound," we begin our journey of faith. It's in this place God will affirm his presence and his power. God wants us to share with others who are searching for truth the joy and peace of no longer being orphaned but of belonging in the family of God. "He wanted us to enter into the celebration of his lavish gift-giving by the hand of his beloved son" (Ephesians1:6, MSG). He wants us to make peace with and resolve our doubts.

Doubt matters

In the upcoming chapters, I pray you will find insight, encouragement, and tools so that you don't have to waver between doubt and belief. Oh, you can doubt. I invite you to grow comfortable with doubting. Alfred, Lord Tennyson says, "There lives more faith in honest doubt, believe me, than in half the creeds."[7] It's not by chance you are reading this book. I am so glad you chose to "doubt your doubts." I pray you have moved closer to belief already and will continue to do so as you read on. Jesus Christ is the answer to "Show me" and "Why me?" God's plans and purpose keep us in the light of his presence. Instead being of spiritually fatherless, you can be reconnected to your perfect heavenly father, who loves to walk with you. He longs to help and guide you through any storm. You will find, as Thomas and I did—and many others—that you really can trust God with your hurts, habits, and hang-ups; he will join you wherever you currently are. Faith is a process. This process can begin and continue at any time.

If you don't know your heavenly father, I pray you will begin your faith journey today. If you have already been on the journey, may it continue in the light of God's love as we roll back the fog of doubt and shine a light on our faith. Remember the godly letter writer and the story of her letters? For sixty-six years Mother Teresa yearned for closeness with God; one wonders why God would hold out on her? I don't think he did. It's in her example to us that we realize that God is present whether we feel his presence or not. He is faithful and will complete what he has started in us as we continue to act and move forward. We must press on and trust that through him things will be okay. Mother Teresa's testimony is a compelling example of continued faith even through periods of doubt.

Frederick Buechner, one of faith's giants, says, "Faith is a way of waiting—never quite knowing, never quite hearing or seeing, because in the darkness we are all but a little lost. There is doubt hard on the heels of every belief, fear hard on the heels of every hope, and many holy things lie in ruins because the world has ruined them and we have ruined them. But faith waits even so, delivered at least from that final despair which gives up waiting altogether because it sees nothing left worth waiting for." (8)

Can you relate?

Listed below are a few statements of truth. Read them over several times today until you believe them for yourself. I can't wait to hear how God encourages you and changes your doubt to belief.

God made me with a need to feel fully alive.
God bridged the gap of spiritual fatherlessness through offering humankind a relationship with his son, Jesus Christ.
God's love covers a multitude of sins.
God can use doubt to help shape my faith.
I can keep going when I don't know the answer to my why.

Chapter 2:

DID GOD HEAR?

"One must know when it is right to doubt, to affirm, and to submit. Anyone who does otherwise does not understand the force of reason." Blaise Pascal

Naveena Shine wanted to find out if she could live on nothing but water for six months. She set out on a mission to explore *breatharianism*, the concept that food is not necessary and sunlight provides all the nourishment the body needs. She was determined to show the world she didn't need to eat. For over a month, she sipped small amounts of water and sucked on ice chips. The sixty-five-year-old UK native ended the extreme self-experiment after forty-seven days because she realized it was "totally dangerous and likely to cause death." Seems like an extreme experiment for an obvious and logical truth.[1]

Sometimes we fast from food or abstain from water purposefully, for health reasons or spiritual discipline, though for much shorter periods of time. When we do, we may feel the need for more acutely afterward. I remember a time of feeling an intense need for liquids after recovering from the stomach flu. My thirst felt unquenchable. I lost track of how often I went to the water dispenser on the door of our refrigerator, filled my glass to the brim, and drank deeply. It's just that easy to do the same with the living water. In John 4, Jesus refers to himself as the living water and says that whoever drinks of him will never be thirsty again. Yet many souls refuse to drink of him because they doubt God's existence or feel they can't trust his love. They remain parched and dry, preferring dehydration to refreshment and slaking their thirsts. It seems many have set out to experiment whether the living water is necessary. Trying to last days, weeks, years without the living water is a type of extreme spiritual breatharianism.

Ravaged and famished

It's easy to recall a time when I felt spiritually parched. For the first time in my life, I was overtaken by lament. This was not just one casual day of shedding a few tears. I'd lost track of the days of anguish. I was doubled over in agony, my flow of emotions uncontrollable. I couldn't stop weeping. I could not understand why I was so depressed. After all, I had a lot of reasons to be happy and even content with my life and should have been satisfied with those I had been given to love. A few years earlier, I had married my college sweetheart, and together we had a beautiful three-year-old daughter, and I was pregnant with our second child. We lived in my husband's hometown, near family, and were settling in to run a family business. Yet every day I had a difficult time getting out of bed. I wondered why God was holding out on me. It felt like God was playing hide-and-seek. I looked to him for answers, direction, and wisdom but heard nothing in return. The relationship with God I once enjoyed, when we walked closely and I shared honestly and felt so comfortable, now felt awkward and cold. Dry. I questioned, *Did God hear my prayers?*

I'd been trying to serve God and live for God for a few years. I was a graduate of a Bible college. I led prayer groups and Bible studies for teenage girls, and my husband was a pastor. I knew how to believe God for other people. In my depression and discouragement, my faith was put to the test when I would pray for others and God would come through. Why? It seemed he was there to work out things for other people. I wasn't convinced God would do the same for me. I wondered, *God, what about me?* I began to distrust God. I thought I had "kept short accounts" with God. Yet I was stuck. I didn't know how to get unstuck. Because of my doubts, I withdrew from him. I did not continue to drink and be satisfied with the only one who could quench my spiritual thirst—the living water.

Job's tests

All believers are tested, and we all pass through difficult times. In scripture, we find Job, a man of God and a prosperous farmer, living with an abundance of property, resources, and family. Satan asks permission of God to attack Job as a way to prove Job's selfish motives. God agrees, and Job responds with faith and to trust in God, modeling for us how we can endure suffering. In Job 2:10, Job asks his wife, "Shall we accept good from God, and not trouble?" As we know, Job was not protected from trouble; when calamity came, he didn't question God's goodness and justice. He persisted in faith, and in the end both his faith and his circumstances were rewarded. God didn't protect Job from bad experiences, nor does he promise us a trouble-free life. Faith in God doesn't guarantee personal prosperity. Lack of faith doesn't guarantee trouble. "He causes his sun to rise on the evil and the good, and sends rain on the righteous and the unrighteous" (Matthew 5:45). God might allow suffering to come for reasons only God understands. Satan's strategy is to undermine our faith to the point of moving from healthy doubting to dangerous disbelief in God's love for us. Job's faith allowed him to accept what he didn't understand, enabling him to live for more than his own comfort. I recalled his example when my faith was tested by depression. I, like Job, hadn't agreed to this cosmic challenge.

The actress

I dug into my depression to learn what the cause was so I could get some relief and discovered something unexpected: I was an actress. Not on the big screen or Broadway, of course, but I expertly manipulated people and situations, putting a cheerful smile on my face to assure everyone all was well, while inside I wished I could die. I hid my real self. I was good at impersonating. On the outside, I appeared professional and appropriate to my roles. After all, I was a pastor's wife, a young mother, and a volunteer in my church. I was nice and agreeable; I didn't make any waves. I let people see only the side of me I wanted them to know. Why? I was a codependent people–pleaser who found delight in setting my feelings aside, even to the point of dishonesty to myself and others. Brennan Manning explains, "Our false self stubbornly blinds each of us to the light and truth of our own emptiness and hollowness. We cannot acknowledge the darkness within."[2]

I was preoccupied with perfectionism, approval, and acceptance. My mind and emotions were stacked to the brim with strongholds. Ed Silvoso says a stronghold is "a mind-set impregnated with hopelessness that causes us to accept as unchangeable situations that we know are contrary to the will of God."[3] Although my initial fath encounter had freed me from bad habits and exposed me to God's healing love, I still had long-buried feelings of shame. I didn't think I deserved to be forgiven. I felt unforgiven, unloved, and ashamed; I felt unworthy and condemned. These lies Satan fed me prevented me from believing God's truth about myself. I knew about the freedom and abundant life God offers us, but I thought it was for everyone else but me. I didn't know that strongholds prevent us from seeing what is true because of how they make us feel. When we are adopted into the family of God, no one erases the "hard drive" of our emotions, memories, or mistakes. We come into the relationship with our heavenly father with false beliefs and coping mechanisms. Neil Anderson says, "Strongholds are mental habit patterns of thought that are not consistent with God's word."[4] Mine needed to be dealt with.

Adversity can strengthen faith by causing us to dig our roots deeper to enable us to withstand the storms. But it can be frightening to live deeper. Living deeper requires time for an honest look at ourselves through the grid of God's word. We must learn how to move away from guilt, shame, and blame, disowning them. We can trust God and expect him to do something good in our lives, and sometimes that good requires us to evict the bad. How? We must not only feed our faith with the word of God, but also learn to declare God's word over ourselves.

Exposed

During my time of deep depression, I wasn't getting well as fast as my husband and I thought I should. I was stuck, unable to address my pain on my own, and so we decided that I would get help. The day my husband, Paul, took me to see a psychologist, my thoughts and emotions bounced all over the place. I was hopeful, yet wary. We had visited other counselors as a couple without success and a few times I'd even gone on my own. I wondered, *Would God come through? He hadn't answered my prayers. Did he love me and want me better? Why would this counselor be any different?*

Terrified, I entered the spacious office; we were welcomed as we settled into roomy leather chairs. After a few moments of gathering background information, the counselor asked, "Why are you here?" I began to sniff, trying to fight back the tears. Then I began to cry, weep, and finally, wail. I couldn't hold it together anymore. Doubled over, head to my knees, I covered my face with my hands and heaved, sobbing uncontrollably. Neither Paul nor the counselor moved toward me. The five or so minutes that passed seemed like an eternity, and then Dr.

Dixon turned my direction and said, "Tell me about your daily life."

Through my sobs, I explained how Paul had asked me to take on more responsibilities with the business. I was now doing both excruciating physical janitorial work and mentally taxing bookkeeping, while taking care of our three-year-old and preparing for the birth of our second child. These physical, mental, and emotional stressors made me tired and unable to cope. They began to reveal areas of spiritually unresolved conflict, much of which involved past illicit sexual experiences. For more than two decades before that meeting, my hurt and hate of those who had wronged me lay buried alive. And now these painful and horrible recollections of people who had taken advantage of me and my feelings of helplessness to defend myself were resurrected by multiple external pressures. In my weakened state, I was vulnerable again. Could I finally come clean and be honest with myself? Would God use the situation not to my harm, but for my good? Marilyn Meberg says, "You gotta feel it to heal it." I wasn't sure I wanted to hurt that good!

Unbeknown to me, God was bringing to the surface issues from my reckless teen years, situations that I had emotionally blocked but that were still harming me from the inside. I didn't directly remember situations, people, or trauma that had robbed me of peace. I didn't want to face or admit to the events that caused my past wounds; I thought these broken and bruised places in my life were better left alone. Buried. But then I knew it was time. God wanted to expose and heal my hurt. I didn't want to face the pain and truth of my past. God wanted to remove the sting of the countless times I had been victimized—to free me. I had difficulty separating my sin from what had been done to me. When I came to grips with the crimes committed against me and stopped owning them and stopped shaming myself for the things which happened without my consent, I began to sense freedom ahead. It was time to be straightforward.

The surgery

The next time I returned for therapy, Dr. Dixon helped me to be brutally honest. This time I was alone. I settled into the leather chair and anxiously gripped the arm. Dr. Dixon asked, "What happened?"

I closed my eyes, wondering where to begin. In my mind's eye, it was like looking down a long hallway with lots of doors to closets that needed to be cleaned out. You know cleaning needs to be done, but which door to open first? I started at the beginning, as far back as I could remember. I was a five-year-old in my first ballet class, feeling uncomfortable in my own skin. The older girls called me demeaning names and bullied me in the locker room. I cringed as I said the specific names aloud that day in Dr. Dixon's office: "Fat-kins. Sausage. Clumsy." The names tumbled out of my mouth, one by one; these titles continued to torment me and again brought me to tears.

The doctor said, "Let it go." It was a relief to finally be rid of my burdensome emotional baggage. I felt lighter immediately.

A few weeks later, I returned to see Dr. Dixon. The Holy Spirit kindly stood next to another closet door; this was another room that needed deep cleaning. I waited as he flung the door open for me to view what was next. Although I had my eyes closed, God brought to mind numerous sexual encounters. It was as if I were watching a video of my activities. My stomach was sick, my head pounded, the images humiliating to think about, not to mention share with another human being. *After all, I am a pastor's wife.* Things became more real as I explained aloud to Dr. Dixon the details of each time I was victimized. I wasn't sure if some of the encounters really happened; I thought they could have been dreams. Yet he encouraged me to remember, describe, and break the sexual bond I had with those involved.

A landmark turn of events was the day the doctor asked, "Was this consensual?" I said, "No." He said, "Then you need to recognize you were taken advantage of, you did not give your permission. It doesn't matter if you were in the wrong place at the wrong time. If you did not want this to happen, you were the victim."

This was freeing news. I couldn't believe it. For so long, I thought these horrible encounters were my fault. Dr. Dixon helped me see which were other people's sins and which were mine and encouraged me to receive the forgiveness offered to me through Jesus Christ. He also helped me to receive forgiveness from myself. "Jesus replied, 'Very truly I tell you, everyone who sins is a slave to sin. Now a slave has no permanent place in the family, but a son belongs to it forever. So if the Son sets you free, you will be free indeed' (John 8:34-36). All of us have things buried or lurking that God wishes to free us from. You may not have been sexually abused, but maybe you were harmed in other ways and have buried those situations and live with the wounds. Those wounds may still fester. These issues, though painful for you to face, are still there, waiting for you to let the light of truth free you. And you can be free. Jesus promises it.

The recovery

If you've ever peeled an onion, you know there are several layers of "skin" before you get to the core. In psychology, the "presenting problem" is the one that takes the client in to see the doctor, but it is usually not why the client is there. "Therapy is the process of getting beyond the original complaint and digging deeper to find out if there are more reasons even more significant than the presenting problem."[5] The process of my healing has taken years, and even today as I write this chapter, I have dealt with a few old lies that have surfaced trying to disguise themselves in new ways so I won't be able to address them—lies making me doubt that I can be freed from shame and live free from pain. One of them is the lie that I am the only one who has gone through this type of anguish. Another is the lie that I don't need to include specific details in this book. And yet another is that no one will want to know what I have gone through or hear the truth that they can also be helped. But now I know freedom comes from exposing lies to the light of truth, and I have done what I know God has asked of me. It's so freeing to know God's word, to speak it over myself and others, face that truth, and let the Holy Spirit heal my wounds. What layers is the Lord peeling back in your life to expose your doubts to the light and heal you?

Warning signs

Like a cancer that can slowly kill us if we don't recognize it and then get treatment, shame and pride our desire to rely only on ourselves for help, may cause us to avoid seeing the "doctor" that can help us relieve our pain. God's will is for us to let go of our past by trusting him with all of our hurts and hang-ups. Letting go is hard—we have been clutching those hurts for so long. I've learned that we can't reach for anything new if our hands are still full of yesterday's junk. I discovered an analogy that was helpful to me along the way toward healing. Our vehicles have safety features, including warning lights to alert us to internal issues. One light comes on if the air in the tires is low. Another light comes on if an oil change is needed. Yet another light comes on if windshield wipers need a fluid refill. My "meltdown" was like a brightly flashing warning light on my emotional dashboard. It was time for me to deal with the areas that I didn't want to address—the hurt and hate that had been buried for decades. How do we deal with them? We understand the truth of our identity in Christ.

The hole made whole

We must understand our identity in Christ (see chart below), this understanding absolutely essential to living the victorious Christian life. No matter what comes our way, in Christ we are secure. Our mistakes should not define us. God doesn't hold our sins, mistakes, or missteps against us. The *real* me is in my identity in Christ. Once we know what God says about us and believe it to be the truth, everything about how we view God and ourselves changes. There's a big difference between who you are in yourself and who you are in Christ. In myself, I am Sheryl Giesbrecht Turner, a woman, wife, mom, daughter, aunt, grandma, employee, and missionary. Writer, speaker, radio and television personality—these are things I do, roles I take on, not who I am. Who I am is who I am *in Christ*.

Dr. Neil T. Anderson says, "Often what we show on the outside is a false front designed to disguise who we really are and cover up the negative feelings we have about ourselves. The world would have us believe that if we appear attractive or perform well or enjoy a certain amount of status, then we will have it all together inside as well. That is not always true; however, external appearance, accomplishment and recognition don't necessarily reflect or produce internal peace or maturity."[6] If we know who we are in Christ, what you are or what you lack doesn't matter anymore. In Christ, you are accepted, you are secure, and you are significant. Once we believe this truth, we can respond to God's everlasting love and, in turn, love ourselves. Why not try it? Speak aloud the truth below, found in God's word, about yourself right now.

Who I Am in Christ

If you are a Christian, then the statements below are true of you.

I am accepted…
John 1:12–I am God's child.
John 15:15–As a disciple, I am a friend of Jesus Christ.

Romans 5:1–I have been justified.

1 Corinthians 6:17–I am united with the Lord, and I am one with him in spirit.

1 Corinthians 6:19-20–I have been bought with a price, and I belong to God.

1 Corinthians 12:27–I am a member of Christ's body.

Ephesians 1:3-8–I have been chosen by God and adopted as his child.

Colossians 1:13-14–I have been redeemed and forgiven of all my sins.

Colossians 2:9-10–I am complete in Christ.

Hebrews 4:14-16–I have direct access to the throne of grace through Jesus Christ.

I am secure...

Romans 8:1-2–I am free from condemnation.

Romans 8:28–I am assured that God works for my good in all circumstances.

Romans 8:31-39–I am free from any condemnation brought against me, and I cannot be separated from the love of God.

2 Corinthians 1:21-22–I have been established, anointed, and sealed by God.

Colossians 3:1-4–I am hidden with Christ in God.

Philippians 1:6–I am confident that God will complete the good work he started in me.

Philippians 3:20–I am a citizen of heaven.

2 Timothy 1:7–I have not been given a spirit of fear but of power, love, and a sound mind.

1 John 5:18–I am born of God and the evil one cannot touch me.

I am significant...

John 15:5–I am a branch of Jesus Christ, the true vine, and a channel of his life.

John 15:16–I have been chosen and appointed to bear fruit.

1 Corinthians 3:16–I am God's temple.

2 Corinthians 5:17-21–I am a minister of reconciliation for God.

Ephesians 2:6–I am seated with Jesus Christ in the heavenly realm.

Ephesians 2:10–I am God's workmanship.

Ephesians 3:12–I may approach God with freedom and confidence.

Philippians 4:13–I can do all things through Christ, who strengthens me.[7]

Truth about me

In some ways, before God exposed my deep wounds, I was like Naveena Shine—the woman who wanted to know if she could survive on no food and only drops of water. I was ravaged by spiritual thirst, dry as a bone, but I didn't realize I could live deeper, doubt my doubts, or declare the truth of God's word over myself. When tested, I turned away from God instead of leaning in to access the well to quench my need for healing. At that time, I didn't have the tools to doubt my doubts or declare the truth of God's word over myself. However, my emotional breakdown and silent suffering offered opportunities for me to find help. Along with professional help through Dr. Dixon, I recieved personal assistance from prayer partners. In the counseling process we dug up past incidents, years of victimization. I didn't want to revisit them because I felt like I'd already suffered enough. But Job's example encouraged me to trust God with his plans, even when they seemed painful and I didn't understand. And yes, we can learn to answer like he did in: "I know that you can do all things; no purpose of yours can be thwarted"(Job 42:4) As I resolved spiritual conflicts, I discovered that the more I consciously considered who I was in Christ, my behavior would confirm my beliefs about God. I acknowledged the process of healing and paid attention to my feelings, allowing God to provide his strength and affirm my wholeness. I wonder, have you asked, *Does God hear me in my pain?* Let me assure you, he does.

Can you relate?

What roles are you playing to cover up your true self?

Are there situations in your past that you need to acknowledge and be freed from?

Which of the statements of truth about your identity in Christ is your favorite?

Share a time when you've waited for an answer from God.

Discuss the answer you received and how God came through.

Chapter 3

NOW WHAT?

"If ours is an examined faith, we should be unafraid to
doubt. If doubt is eventually justified, we were believing what clearly was not worth believing. But if doubt is
answered, our faith has grown stronger. I know God more
certainly and I can enjoy God more deeply. There is no
believing without some doubting, and believing is all the
stronger for understanding and resolving doubt."[1]
Os Guinness

Grand Banks, Newfoundland, is the foggiest
place in the world. Off the Canadian coastline, it's where a
chilly current from the north meets up with the much warm-
er Gulf Stream from the south. The result is an impenetrable
206 foggy days per year. The fog begins burning off inland and
slowly dissipates toward the coastline, so it seems as if the fog
never actually leaves. [2] There's no doubt that there is something

about the way fog can change how a landscape appears simply by enveloping it in a cloud. Thick fog can deceive us, especially by limiting our visibility. In the same way, unsure, unstable life conditions can distort our view with a haze of uncertainty. We can feel dazed and uncomfortable and begin to distrust God's direction because we can't see where he is leading.

Fogged in

In March 2004 I found a small lump underneath my left eye. At first I thought it was due to allergies since we live in an agricultural valley with planting, pruning, and harvesting, so I increased my allergy medication. The lump grew. I then thought I could have developed an allergic reaction to my eye makeup, so I threw my mascara out. The lump grew a bit more. After two months, the lump pushed my lower left eyelid up so that it blocked the lower half of my eye. Two of my girlfriends said, "Sheryl, you really need to get that checked out." And so, finally, I made an appointment at my medical system's urgent care. The general practice doctor's face grew taut as she poked and prodded the lump. As she examined me, she asked if I was overly tired, or unusually nauseated and where on a scale of one to ten did my pain register. At the end of the exam, I knew there was something very wrong. She referred me to an ophthalmologist who sent me for more tests, including an MRI of my head. As I traveled from doctor to doctor, fear and worry descended over me, encasing me in a thick haze. Dread and anxiousness caused me to question God and his provision, and this doubt opened a door for defense mechanisms such as self-pity, discouragement, anger, and even depression to flood in. This was a time of wondering what was wrong with me, and my security in Christ was tested. I had taught scriptural truths about our identity in Christ scriptural truths to women's groups, at conferences, and in churches across the United States. All I wanted to do was serve God, and now this? Although I knew the Lord had all my trials and tests in hand, this was one I had not anticipated, and that old enemy, doubt, began to creep in once more. Doesn't it always when unexpected and bad news arrives?

The results of the MRI showed a lump that was contained in the lower part of the lymph node of the eyelid, which was good in some ways—it wasn't a brain tumor or a hematoma. In tandem with the MRI, I'd had additional blood work done. These varied and exclusive examinations did not reveal anything abnormal, but the ophthalmologist ordered a biopsy of the lump.

It was a very long two weeks before our follow-up appointment with the ophthalmologist, who reviewed the biopsy results with us. Paul and I were shocked when the doctor said, "You have lymphoma…cancer." Our jaws dropped at the same time. We were devastated. Paul's family tree had roots that went deep into cancer diagnoses, and treatment. Each person who'd faced the disease passed away. But there was no cancer in my family. I asked God, *Why me?* We wondered if God had gotten the wrong Giesbrecht.

We were referred to an oncologist, and as the reality of the cancer diagnosis began to sink in, I made poor choices that made my life more difficult. I decided to do a little Google search on "stage four non-Hodgkin's lymphoma" and made the unfortunate discovery that my future was not very bright. I was shocked to find there was a 68-70% chance I would not recover! The chemotherapy prescribed for me was a trial, and there were no guarantees it would work. I took this newfound information on as a challenge. I decided to visualize my recovery and healing. I saw myself on the other side of the treatments and in the positive, healed, cancer-free 30-32% of survivors. Instead of accepting a doom-and-gloom cancer diagnosis, I chose to take on the battle. After all, cancer is just a name, right? I made a choice right then to allow God to fight this physical battle with cancer. I would take up my authority in Christ and stand firm in who God said I was: I am accepted, I am secure, and I am significant. I was reminded of 1 Peter 1:7, Which reads, "These trials will show that your faith is genuine. It is being tested as fire tests and purifies gold—though your faith is far more precious than mere gold. So when your faith remains strong through many trials, it will bring you much praise and glory and honor on the day when Jesus Christ is revealed to the whole world" (NLT).

Limited vision

The next week we met our new oncologist, Dr. Risbud. He took pride in explaining details about treatment, side effects, and recovery to his patients and showed us the PET scan images on a screen. Dr. Risbud used his pen to point to places on the film. Beginning at the spot under my left eye, he moved the pen to show the areas the cancer had invaded: the bone marrow of my right arm, the shoulder and elbow of my right arm, and the femur of my left leg. Dr. Risbud said, "You have stage four non-Hodgkin's lymphoma." Because of my internet research, we were very aware of the seriousness of the diagnosis.

It was a sweltering hot day in July as I began my first of eight cycles of chemotherapy. I took only one book with me: *A Bend in the Road* by Dr. David Jeremiah. Dr. Jeremiah had fully recovered from the same kind of cancer, not just once, but twice. He called his cancer a disruptive moment. He writes, "The moment we accept the fact that our ordeal has been permitted, even intended by God, our perspective on disruptive moments will totally change."[3] So we chose to see this trial as a small bump in the road, a disruptive moment, a lesson God permitted to allow us to grow closer to him. Disruptive moments are opportunities for God to strengthen us and deepen our faith if we let him. They are opportunities to place our trust in an all-knowing God rather than rely on our limited human perspective. God strengthen us and deepen our faith and trust in God and not solely on the human approach to things. When that strength is enshrined in weakness, there is power in pain; spiritual, emotional, and physical pain can lead us to a stronger faith in God's power. That's why disruptive moments can glorify God.

Change my name

In the book of Ruth, Naomi also had a disruptive moment or two. Naomi's world fell apart. Naomi's husband died and then both of her sons died. Naomi entered into a season of doubting God's love. She was a broken woman, depressed and discouraged. She lived in a strange land, among her enemies, her husband and sons all dead. She was a widow, unable to support herself, without a future or hope. Widows in her day usually supported themselves by prostitution or became beggars. Naomi didn't hide how she was feeling. In Ruth 1:20-21, after returning to her home, she responded to the women calling her name: "Don't call me Naomi," she told them. "Call me Mara, because the Almighty has made my life very bitter. I went away full, but the Lord has brought me back empty. Why call me Naomi? The Lord has afflicted me; the Almighty has brought misfortune upon me." God was not surprised by Naomi's feelings. We can doubt our doubts, ask ourselves if they are true or valid, without living a doubting way of life. When we are honest with God, we give a name to how we feel. This is what Naomi did when she said, "Call me Mara (bitter)." Naomi's feelings lied to her, yet as she spoke her thoughts aloud, God provided encouragement to her through Ruth. Angela Perrett says, "Like Naomi, we allow our emotions to dictate truth to us instead of God's word. We allow our emotions and our hurt to cloud our eyesight and we fail to see how God is providing for our needs in the midst of our pain."[4] The remedy for that is to review the truth of our identity in Christ. As we renew our minds through the power of God's word, we can tell our emotions to bow down to the truth. We choose to respond according to the reality of our faith.

The raw reality

My first chemotherapy treatment was just like out of a medical text book. The week before, I stopped by the lab for necessary blood work and then had my pre-operation appointment with the surgeon for the Port-a-Cath insertion. The following day the nurse discussed the procedure with me and showed me a video about the expected side effects of chemotherapy. I found out that the chemotherapy Dr. Risbud prescribed was created out of mouse protein; it was cutting edge and had been on the market only three years. Mouse protein? Weird. The mixture of drugs sounded a little strange, but I didn't question anything he prescribed. I wanted to be a good patient and do what my doctor told me to do. Of course, we prayed for wisdom for Dr. Risbud in choosing which drug therapy would work and for the cancer to respond in a positive way to the medication. We decided to make the best of my bleak situation with humor. Paul, my teenage son Ben, and I looked on the bright side of our situation and named it *tumor humor.* We came up with our own mouse jokes, which kept grins on our faces even on the darkest days. Our nurse said, "Expect your chemo to last anywhere from eight to twelve hours. Since it is your first one, we use very small amounts and it goes through the IV very slowly, which can take a while. Also, expect the chemo to send you into shock. It might not happen, but be ready if it does."

During the first treatment, just as Nurse Roger had suggested might happen, I had a reaction to the medication. It felt like someone was sitting on my chest, and I began gasping for air. I mouthed the words, "I can't breathe," and Roger turned down the dosage. In a few seconds my breathing returned to normal. And then I told him, "I have this unusual craving to build a nest and eat cheese." He said, "I think your tail was trying to grow too fast." We laughed, giggled, and smiled, and that sure made the chemotherapy go smoother—or at least made us yearn for the next snack. As the months went by, people sent us mouse cards and funny mice items, and my sister-in-law even gave me a pair of Mickey Mouse ears. I had a list of invites to go to Starbucks for cheese and crackers. I knew this battle was one I could not fight on my own. Paul put together a prayer list and emailed it out to concerned prayer warriors around the world as we learned the truth of 1 Corinthians 13:12: "For now we see through a glass, darkly; but then face to face: now I know in part; but then shall I know even as also I am known" (KJV). God took me to a deeper place with him. He asked me to learn lessons. These were lessons I could not learn any other way except during the season of lymphoma. So I asked him to teach me. I wanted to learn the "lessons of lymphoma" so I could come through and on the other side of it. I was surprised at what I learned—that there are some hard places we all must walk through to overcome doubt.

Doubt your doubts

"We can doubt our doubts without having to live a doubting way of life. Doubt encourages rethinking. Its purpose is more to sharpen the mind than to change it. Doubt can be used to pose the question, get an answer, and push for a decision. But doubt was never meant to be a permanent condition. Doubt is one foot lifted, poised to step forward or backward. There is no motion until the foot comes down." [5] The decision is a commitment to trust God no matter what life brings our way, accepting that in both good and bad circumstances, God knows what's best for us.

Naomi and her widowed daughter-in-law Ruth spent some time waiting before they left Moab. They eventually decided to return to Naomi's homeland of Bethlehem. Ruth was committed to staying with her mother-in-law and embraced Naomi's God, the God of Israel as her Lord. The women, both widows, could expect only difficult times ahead of them, and yet God had a delightful surprise for them as they moved forward through doubtful times in faith. Naomi knew that when a woman's husband died, the law allowed to marry a brother of her dead husband. Because Naomi had no more sons to offer to Ruth, the nearest relative could take his place. Naomi knew the law in Deuteronomy 25:5-10 stating that the kinsman-redeemer was to be responsible for the extended family. In their extended family, that kinsman-redeemer, a near male relative, was Boaz. He had the right to redeem Naomi by marrying Ruth. Both Naomi and Ruth would have to wait for God's provision—as would I.

Foghorn

Within the first three days after my chemotherapy, I noticed the size of the lump had become much smaller. Since we lived near the doctor's office, I stopped by without an appointment to show him. I had a captive audience right there in the office with the doctor and nurses, all extremely excited to see that, indeed, the chemo was working. I was thankful for the decreasing lump—outward evidence of the effectiveness of the medication.

There were many more blessings heaped on us through the body of Christ, our Sunday school class, and our church family at Olive Drive Church. Not only were people in Kern County praying, but saints across the nation and around the world prayed for me. I received hundreds of encouraging phone calls, and I have a binder full of emails and a dresser full of cards. We enjoyed lunches and dinners and baked goods prepared especially for us, according to my restricted dietary needs. Friends provided housecleaning, ran errands, bought and wrapped Christmas gifts and wrapping, and mailed Christmas cards for me. There were also numerous gifts of prayer quilts, flowers, plants, books, bracelets, clothes—and even a Cher wig! Many days I would be lying on my couch exhausted when I'd get a phone call and someone would say, "Can I bring you dinner?"

The final PET scan was on January 19, 2005. Dr Risbud, excited about the outcome, called me on January 20 to say, "Sheryl, I can't believe it—the cancer is totally gone!" Like Dr. Jeremiah writes in *A Bend in the Road*: "Our prayer should be: God, you have allowed this in my life. I don't understand it, but I know that it couldn't have happened to me unless it was filtered through your loving hands. So this thing is from you."[6] That's a very difficult prayer to pray, isn't it?

Make adjustments

That is what Ruth did. Ruth gleaned in the fields of Naomi's relative, Boaz, who out of compassion for the widowed women, allowed Ruth to glean and also purposely left extra grain. Ruth told Naomi she had gleaned extra grain from Boaz's fields. Naomi's response is given in Ruth 2:20: "'The Lord bless him!' Naomi said to her daughter-in-law. 'He has not stopped showing his kindness to the living and the dead.'

She added, 'That man is our close relative; he is one of our kinsman-redeemers.'" Naomi understood God's provision and received God's blessing. When we know God's word, we can claim his promises, and they will help us forge forward into an unknown future. Naomi's faith was blessed as Boaz took the role of the kinsman-redeemer; Ruth became his wife, thus providing for their future and ours, too. Ruth's marriage to Boaz impacted the genealogy of Christ through the birth of their son, Obed. God truly gave them hope and a future! My disruptive moments were redeemed when we saw that God had them in hand all along. A turning point for me, for Naomi, and for you, if you so choose, can come when we look to God and accept his will.

Ruth 4:14-15 says, "The women said to Naomi: 'Praise be to the Lord, who this day has not left you without a kinsman-redeemer. May he become famous throughout Israel! He will renew your life and sustain you in your old age. For your daughter-in-law, who loves you and who is better to you than seven sons, has given him [Obed] birth.'" Naomi praised God as he provided for her after tragedy.

Fog warning

Wouldn't it be great if we were warned about uncomfortable circumstances we are destined to face in life? I live in the Central Valley of California. We have fog, and although it's nothing like Grand Banks, Newfoundland, there are extreme fog conditions in our winter months. The "dense fog advisory" report lets us know details before we take the road or send the kids off to school. Recently while driving on the freeway in intense fog, with the usual congestion of morning traffic, I had to slow down to 35 miles per hour. There was a car ahead with its emergency flashers on. At first, it looked like the car was disabled, and we thought, what a terrible time and place to break down. But as we came closer, we saw that the car was cautiosuly traveling less than 30 miles per hour in the fast lane, flashers on, no doubt petrified about driving with such little visibility. We were forced to go around it. In our landlocked valley, we learn to pay attention to three things: visibility, timing, and impacts. As we travel, the fog obscures our view and we must proceed with caution. Most of the time we can see only a few feet ahead. We must travel slowly but steadily, by faith, believing that the way is clear, that other people will drive safely, and that all the safety precautions are in place.

Spiritually, there is a parallel here to what we must choose to do. Do you think God is taking too long? He wants us to wait in faith but move slowly forward. "That is why I wait expectantly, trusting God to help, for he has promised" (Psalm 130:5, TLB). We must trust him—that's called belief. "Believe in the Lord your God, and you will be able to stand firm" (2 Chronicles 20:20, NLT). When he wins the victory, we can celebrate. "Then all the men returned to Jerusalem, with Jehoshaphat leading them, overjoyed that the Lord had given them victory over their enemies" (2 Chronicles 20:27, NLT).

If we let God fight our battles, there is no question who will win. We need to believe God will conquer our foes and transform our doubts into even stronger belief. Our natural reaction is to look at the magnitude of our problems; we focus on the problem and not the solution. If this is our method, we fight our battles using the temporary quick-fix methods of the world—words with pat answers, fad diets, and worldly advice or we even ignore another person's emotional pain so that we don't have to deal with it, or them. But if we submit to God and commit a person or situation to God's plans—stop, stand still, wait, and believe—we show that we expect God to work. When the victory comes, it will be obvious it came from God. Then, we celebrate. Rick Warren says, "The deepest level of worship is praising God in spite of pain, thanking God during a trial, trusting him when tempted, surrendering while suffering, and loving him when he seems distant."[7] What a comfort that God knows even our path of suffering; our goal during suffering is to let God refine us.

Can you relate?
What or who are you waiting on?
What's your current disruptive moment?
How will you adjust your perspective to align it with God's today?
What lessons are you learning?

Chapter 4:

NOT SURE

"With great doubts come great understanding; with little
doubts come little understanding." Chinese proverb

"My coming to faith did not start with a leap but
rather a series of staggers from what seemed like one safe place
to another," Anne Lamott writes in *Traveling Mercies*. "Like
lily pads, round and green, these places summoned and then
held me up while I grew. Each prepared me for the next leaf on
which I would land, and in this way, I moved across the swamp
of doubt and fear."

Famous novelist, teacher, and speaker, Lamott has written
about her struggles with doubt in several of her novels. "I have a
lot of faith. But I am also afraid a lot and have no real certainty
about anything," she writes. "I remembered something Father
Tom had told me—that the opposite of faith is not doubt, but
certainty. Certainty is missing the point entirely. Faith includes

noticing the mess, the emptiness and discomfort, and letting it be there until some light returns."[1]

Like Ms. Lamott, after completing my final chemo, I moved from one safe place on the road to my physical recovery to the next one. Each time I completed a full blood workup, finished a CAT scan, or finalized a full-body PET scan with results showing no cancer, I knew I was moving forward. It was the answer we wanted—my total and complete healing! I learned about God's will for my recovery, allowing the saints in my family, friendship circle, and church to serve me, while allowing myself to share my honest feelings. These "lessons of lymphoma" strengthened me, preparing me for the next shroud of disbelief, which came all too quickly. Like Anne Lamott, I was about to learn that the opposite of faith is certainty, and if we also look to recognize God at work when things don't turn out as we hope they will, he will make our faith strong. It took walking through the most heartrending experience in my life to understand this.

Worst nightmare

"Paul didn't make it." The emergency room doctor strained to give me the bad news. "He had a heart attack in the helicopter. The EMTs used the paddles on him, but he did not survive. Paul has died." My beloved husband's unconscious and battered body had been taken away after a horrible motorcycle accident by emergency helicopter only a few hours earlier. I wasn't allowed to ride along with my precious cargo, so after a two-hour drive, I arrived at the hospital—cold, alone, and fearful. Persistent doubts about God haunted me: *If God really loved me, then why did Paul die?*

I could not take in this unbelievable news. It had been a short five years since Paul had sat beside me in a prayer vigil during the long hours of my chemotherapy treatments as together we battled my stage IV cancer. The devastating and horrifying news of his sudden death set my emotions into a tailspin, caused my vision to blur and my mind to freeze. The heart attack resulting from the motorcycle accident, not my cancer, had become my worst nightmare. I was numb. The truth loomed—Paul was gone.

"No!" I screamed as I fell to the floor. "There must be some mistake. It can't be true." But the doctors confirmed the truth: Paul was dead. I couldn't believe it. Paul had been so physically fit, in good health with no heart issues, the motorcylcle accident had produced multiple traumatic injuries, resulting in the heart attack that ushered him into heaven. Paul: my husband, pastor, and ministry partner was dead. My senses numbed as I tried to get a handle on reality; I struggled to process the newly presented facts. Going forward into a future without Paul didn't make sense. The magnitude of this tragedy was too much to take in. In the midst of it all, I remembered the scripture passage I had taught not more than eight hours earlier. The words gnawed on my raw emotions: "'For I know the plans I have for you,' declares the Lord, 'plans to prosper you and not to harm you, plans to give you hope and a future'" (Jeremiah 29:11). My head was clouded and cluttered with chaos. I became overcome by fear, uncertainty, and agony. Questions loomed. How could Paul's death "prosper" me? The Hebrew word for prosperity means "a good and hoped for outcome."[2] At that moment, I didn't get what I'd hoped for on earth, but spiritually could I anticipate God's hope? How could I sort through my doubts, fears, questions, and curiosities to continue to live a productive life? I felt smothered by distrust. I wanted so much to believe. In that dark moment, my own misgivings and skepticism hid the truth of God's hope.

A few years earlier, everything had worked out exactly as hoped for with my cancer. But nothing I'd hoped for occurred with Paul's accident. Could I find hope and move forward from secure place to secure place, even when the future looked bleak? Maybe you've not lost a loved one. But you do have losses, even if they are different: your job ended, your marriage changed, or perhaps you moved to a new city and had to start over. Everyone must push through trials and darkness. We've begun to understand how God can reclaim our past, to help us see beyond the fog and actually allow disruptions as tools to build our faith, but most of us still need reminders of God's goodness and presence. I've found it helps to review our own experiences, as well as the challenges and ultimate successes of others, to allow hope to light our way.

God's plan

When things are hard, some of us are prone to spend a lot of time questioning God's plans for us. What if his plans don't meet with our approval? It's good to consider the plans God has for us, but as we do, we must remember, "It's not all about us." In light of God's grand design, everything in our lives is very small. Even the changes we face are minuscule compared to the majesty of God's plan. But how do we keep ourselves focused on this truth. Let's look to a beloved Bible hero for an example.

Reluctant warrior

Gideon was a notable doubter. Gideon asked God, "Why me?" He wasn't sure about God's call on his life. Can you relate? He, too, questioned God about the problems he and his nation faced and about God's apparent lack of help. The angel of the Lord appeared to Gideon in Judges 6:12: "When the angel of the Lord appeared to Gideon, he said, 'The Lord is with you, mighty warrior.' Gideon's response was honest. 'Sir,' Gideon replied, 'if the Lord is with us, why has all this happened to us? And where are all the miracles that our ancestors told us about? Didn't they say, "The Lord brought us up out of Egypt"? But now the Lord has abandoned us and handed us over to the Midianites'" (Judges 6:13, NLT).

The Israelites had brought calamity upon themselves when they decided to disobey and neglect God. They did not have an open discussion in which they sought understanding and then pushed past their doubts. Thus, they suffered the consequences of unbelief: they worshiped idols and were turned over to the hands of the Midianites (Judges 6:1). In contrast, Gideon had an honest discussion with God. He was willing to ask the difficult questions. Gideon struggled with an inferiority complex. He doubted that God could use him to turn the tide against Israel's oppressors. He tested God. Not once, but twice. Remember the fleece? Gideon demanded extra signs from God. Although this was bold, it was evidence of doubt. Visible signs are unnecessary, but in a moment of fear or weakness, they might confirm what we already know is true. God humored Gideon and gave him a sign, which allayed Gideon's fears and took him from doubt to belief. Through Gideon, God led the Israelites to victory.

Remarkably, God reduced Gideon's army from 32,000 to 300. When God then used Gideon to lead the Israelites to victory, there was no question that God had given them the power to win. Like Gideon, we must recognize the danger of fighting in our own strength during our moments of questioning. We can be confident of victory only if we put our trust and confidence in God and not in ourselves. Gideon was willing to look at his own weaknesses and get out of the way to let God fight his battle. Sometimes we might face calamities resulting from our actions, like the Israelites; sometimes our troubles stem from difficult circumstances. Often we don't have any say about the trials we face, so our job is to bring our doubts and fears to God in honesty and let him respond.

We shouldn't be afraid to talk about our doubts with God and others. It was, and continues to be, an encouragement for me to test my doubts; Anne Lamott did the same thing during her times of questioning God. In the same way, Gideon expressed his doubt to God, opening the door to understanding, and doing so helped him have the God-confidence he needed to lead the Israelites to victory. If we don't express our doubts, we deprive ourselves of an opportunity that can lead to God's response and our doubts being solved.

Farewell for now

After the doctors told me that Paul was dead, I left the hospital with many doubts. But I had learned to express them. *God, what is going on? I survived stage IV cancer, Paul and I fought it together, and now Paul is dead. Don't you love me, our family, our future?* Pastor Paul Giesbrecht's motorcycle accident was horrific, unexpected, tragic. It was my worst nightmare. I was the one to find him, a crumpled heap by the side of the road, fewer than five minutes after the crash. The worst part was the helplessness I felt as his life slipped away from me. In the past, we'd faced many other difficulties, and I'd been able to fix most anything. But the fatal injuries he sustained that day won. Paul had been the love of my life, my college sweetheart, a devoted husband for almost three decades, the father of my two children, my speaking and writing coach, best friend, and pastor. I lost them all in one moment. There was no happy ending here as there had been with my cancer.

That fateful day I began a blind trek down a lonely road through the valley of the shadow of death. I became a widow and a single parent, and my children were now fatherless. I learned not only about death and dying but also about griev-ing. I learned my crazy feelings of grief were normal. I found out that grief is like an uninvited houseguest who won't go away. I discovered only I could grieve my own grief in my own way. The most important thing I learned was how to be honest with myself. Although I didn't want to feel my losses, anguish, and pain, I discovered how to be in touch with my feelings and not deny them. The process was excruciatingly painful, just like the earlier emotional surgery with Dr. Dixon had been. It took time for me to heal, but once I understood my feelings, I found that it helped if I communicated them to others who wanted to share my burden. Although I didn't know how I could find the way through that darkness and despair, God had proved him-self to me in the past. I was going to have to trust his unfailing love, his constant faithfulness, and his strong presence. Thankfully, I had a "teacher" to follow—Gideon.

Victorious warrior

Gideon showed us a process to follow if we have seasons of doubt. He didn't stay stuck in his doubt but instead allowed the Lord to bring him to the point of acceptance and belief. It helps to come before God in prayer; when we bring our doubts to him, we must be very specific about the doubts and requests we have. Gideon honestly questioned God in Judges 6:15: "'Pardon me, my lord,' Gideon replied, 'but how can I save Israel? My clan is the weakest in Manasseh, and I am the least in my family.'" Candor is crucial as we share our thoughts. Don't worry; God can handle them.

Like Gideon, I shared my honest feelings with the Lord. Early on, I told him I didn't think it was fair that Paul got to go to heaven first. We'd always been so competitive, and now Paul was "promoted" while I was left behind to take care of our ministry alone. God brought to mind Ecclesiastes 7:1: "A good name is better than fine perfume, and the day of death better than the day of birth" and Psalm 139:16: "Your eyes saw my unformed body; all the days ordained for me were written in your book before one of them came to be." These verses brought comfort and hope to me, provided grounding to increase my faith, and gave me the peace God promises.

Acknowledging doubts is the first step. Then we must refuse to settle into doubts, choosing to move forward belief. It helps to find someone who is safe, someone we can share our doubts with aloud. Silent doubts rarely find answers. Philippians 4:6-7 tells us, "Do not be anxious about anything, but in every situation, by prayer and petition, with thanksgiving, present your requests to God. And the peace of God, which transcends all understanding, will guard your hearts and your minds in Christ Jesus." God will help us, if we are willing to see him as he really is and be present where he really is. I discovered even in the midst of my tragedy that he was present, available, providing hope and even healing as I kept my eyes on him instead of on my losses.

Author Jerry Bridges says, "We are deceived when we choose to see God other than he is."[3] Our view of God can be covered or clouded by our circumstances or our twisted way of processing events. Research shows that in our early childhood we form attitudes and beliefs in two primary ways. First, we form attitudes through prevailing our circumstances such as our family, our neighborhood, and our schools. The second way we develop our attitudes is through traumatic experiences, such as the death of a family member or favorite pet, relocation to a new city, the divorce of our parents, or any mental or physical abuse. Dr. Neil T. Anderson says, "We are not in bondage to traumatic experiences; we are in bondage to the lies we believed as a result of those experiences."[4]

While our minds can hear that circumstances have changed a current situation, it takes up to six months for our hearts to catch up to the reality. If we have a new reality or a sudden life interruption, our first reaction usually is to switch into "survival mode." It took months for my new reality to sink in. My mind knew Paul was gone, but my heart kept expecting him to return home from a trip, to walk through our front door.

Healthy adjustment comes when we allow our heart time to catch up with what our minds know to be true. Life offers opportunities to doubt or believe God through many unwanted circumstances, and you will find him present, faithful, and true in all of them.

Can you relate to any difficult circumstances on this list? Please add your own challenging situations too.

Disease: Lupus, fibromyalgia, cancer, and others.

Denial or Doubt: I want to believe God, but I just can't.

Depression: I can't get out of bed.

Destruction: 911 calls, a fiscal cliff, natural disasters, a shooting.

Despair: Why am I here?

Divorce: I wanted to stay married, but he did not.

Discouragement: I pray the same prayer over and over, but nothing changes.

Domestic violence: It's my secret; I am the silent sufferer.

Death: I never expected to bury him/her.

There is no denying these situations are grueling. We can choose to move through circumstances and doubt without being deceived into thinking that difficulties happen because God doesn't love us, deciding to then move away from him. Choosing spiritual fatherlessness is never the answer. When we choose to believe God's truth, our new and perhaps unwelcome reality can be God's open door for us to walk through and even embrace the new adventures he has in store. God will not change his mind about his plans and purpose for us; we can be certain of them as we trade our doubts for the truth we of his word. How do we do this? Scripture, friends, and wise counsel.

Keep moving

The day after Paul died, our dear friend and grief specialist, Dr. H. Norman Wright, stopped by my home, bringing me multiple copies of his book *Experiencing Grief*. That night I couldn't sleep, so I picked up the little book and read it cover to cover in about an hour. My mind was distracted, struggling to connect the memory of the accident with my new reality. A certain line attributed to Barbara Baumgartner helped me to process: "Grief is a statement—a statement that you loved someone."[5] This truth permitted me to grieve as we waded through writing a eulogy, picking a coffin, and planning a burial service. It helped me understand that it was okay to feel weird about preparing to say good-bye. While making those preparations, we had permission to laugh, cry, remember, and ready ourselves to help others honor Paul's legacy of love.

Several weeks later, Paul's memorial service was completed. The graveside service was a memory, the last bit of company gone. I was relieved to have the house to myself finally, yet I didn't want to be alone. After the houseguests vacated, so did my emotions. I had been off work for a month, yet I wasn't ready to see anyone. I wasn't ready to be seen. I needed God to be real, near, and present. Yet God seemed so disconnected and aloof. I remembered a similarly difficult experience a few years earlier as Dr. Dixon had encouraged me to face my past sexual trauma. Portions of these two times were comparable—my emotions were raw, yet numb, in both situations as I searched for God during my grief. At times it seemed as if God were keeping himself from me. I knew this wasn't true. I had to keep turning to God's word and to the comforters he sent to my side to tell me the truth. But their telling the truth to me wasn't enough; I had to keep telling myself the truth.

Realizing that was more than a feeling and later, look-ing back, I saw how God was close to me both times. While grieving Paul, I stumbled across verses that helped me during the times I felt as if I couldn't see. "I will lead the blind by ways they have not known, along unfamiliar paths I will guide them; I will turn the darkness into light before them and make the rough places smooth. These are the things I will do; I will not forsake them" (Isaiah 42:16). God gave this scripture to me during the time doubt blinded me. This beautiful truth and many more kept me from turning my back on God. The verse gave me confidence that he would be with me, direct me, and take me gently forward. It didn't matter if the doubt made me feel blind; God had a hold on me, his presence gave me comfort, and his wisdom gave me hope. 2 Chronicles 16:9 states, "For the eyes of the LORD range throughout the earth to strengthen those whose hearts are fully committed to him."

Side by side

As the days and months went by, it was surprising to ob-serve those who walked with me through the grief as well as disappointing and sad to notice those who couldn't handle the journey. I expected certain people to text, email, call, or come over and was disappointed when they weren't available to sup-port my children or me. I grew deeply angry, embittered, and even hateful of those who seemed not to care about Paul's loss of life or our future. Dr. H. Norman Wright invited me to come to his office to talk about my feelings. At first, I vented my disgust and resentment to him twice a week. It felt good to get rid of this type of emotional sewage, especially when my grief was fresh and my wounds were gaping. He said, "Sheryl, you must let go of your anger or it will eat you alive." I began the process of going deeper with God again through this season of grief. Each week that I saw Norm, it seemed as if the clouds of despair lifted a little more. Still cautious and hesitant, I began to feel better about my future as I grew willing to express my doubt, anger, and grief, instead of bottling it up. My hope was renewed as I began to make positive choices.

My church was hosting a GriefShare[6] seminar in January. GriefShare is a grief recovery group that includes a teaching DVD with a note-taking outline, daily personal journal opportunities, and small group discussion. I wasn't sure if the curriculum would help me because I'd heard that for some people it was too emotionally painful to complete the thirteen-week program. I signed up despite my doubts. Have you ever stepped out in uncertainty when you weren't sure it was right? We have much to learn from another well-loved and familiar Bible character who knew grief well.

Death's door

King David sinned against God. He had an affair that resulted in a crisis pregnancy with Bathsheba, and then he planned and participated in the murder of her husband, Uriah. David then wove a detailed plan of deception to cover his tracks. The prophet Nathan exposed the king's flaws and predicted the consequences: death for the newborn child. King

David wrote Psalm 51 during this time, petitioning God to change his mind. David's circumstances were brought on by his sin, but when God worked his plan and not David's, the result was intense grief, a grief with which I could identify. The passage records David's honest feelings toward the sins he committed against God in a bold confession and with a contrite heart: "Have mercy on me, O God, according to your unfailing love; according to your great compassion blot out my transgressions. Wash away all my iniquity and cleanse me from my sin" (Psalm 51:1-2).

Before his infant son's death, David had to face the awful consequences of his sin. In 2 Samuel 12:16, "David pleaded with God for the child. He fasted and spent the nights lying in sackcloth on the ground." God heard his cries, yet God's plan was not to heal the child. The child died. David then dried his eyes and moved past his grief and doubt to serve and trust God with the future.

In the same way, I dried my eyes and moved past my grief and doubt to trust God. To do so, I had to let go of what I thought was best for my life. Although neither Paul nor I had sinned, God had allowed his plan—the one not to heal Paul—to prevail, and the result was my intense grief. I learned that even and perhaps especially when we are not at fault as was David, doubts arise when God doesn't do things our way. I had planned to serve God for the rest of my life together with Pastor Paul. I chose to let go of those expectations and plans. I decided to focus on healing.

I had tentatively decided to attend the GriefShare support group. I had my doubts about going because I knew only one person—our leader. I didn't want strangers meddling in my life. I'd started over in a new church and wondered if I would have the energy or the emotions to let these unfamiliar people join my grief journey. That first night I was running late, my stomach in knots and my head pounding with a splitting headache, yet I was determined to at least greet the leader of the group. I very much needed direction and purpose, a place I could learn to walk the journey of grief, supported along the way. I was curious how this might work, so I moved forward.

Absolute certainty

Although I didn't know the way through grief, just like Anne Lamott tiptoed on the lily pads of her questions, and Gideon hesitated as he moved forward, I stepped from one place of healing to the next. I rediscovered the truth of what I had previously experienced—that God is enough. He showed his provisions to my family and me through his people. Close family, heartfelt friends, and even people I didn't know well tangibly heaped God's love on us in creative ways. Over the course of days, months, and years, there were meals in my refrigerator and freezer, phone calls, emails and cards; some friends even sent one card every week for a whole year. For several years, every six months, one sweet friend sent red roses on the seventeenth of the month, the date of the anniversary of Paul's death. God's love evidenced through the saints, truly wrapped itself around our circumstances, and one day I was able to hear God's voice and feel him again. At the end of our GriefShare group's remembrance service, I honored Paul's legacy and memory through sharing my journey with the dear saints in the support group.

Are you unsure of stepping out into new territory? Let me assure you, the first step is the most difficult. Although I'd begun to wade through my doubt and grief, because this was the most traumatizing thing I'd ever experienced, I would soon find out God had more to show me. Throughout the rest of this book, I hope to show you how God led me to hope in a new life after the death of my husband so that you, too, may have new hope in whatever circumstances you face.

Can you relate?

What situation are you facing that is forcing you to both doubt and then trust God?

Has this circumstance caused you to see God other than he really is?

Have you seen God in his word, in spending time with your family, or in the wise counsel of friends?

Is it time for you to let go of the doubt and step from one safe spot to the next, moving forward?

Chapter 5

I'M AFRAID

"Knowledge and doubt are inseparable to man. The sole alternative to 'knowledge-with-doubt' is no knowledge at all. Only God and certain madmen have no doubts!"
Martin Luther[1]

A common attraction at our local county fair is the house of mirrors. When you walk into the exhibit, you see your reflection "rearranged," depending on the shape of the mirror's width or height. One mirror makes you appear dwarf-like, while another makes you appear tall and skinny, like a bean pole. As you look at your distorted image, you are deceived or may even be frightened by what you see in the mirror; the person reflected is certainly not as he or she appears.

Although we appreciate the house of mirrors as comic relief, the popular attraction is a tangible spiritual illustration of how we can be misled into believing something other than what is true about God. Satan can keep us ensnared in doubt, deception, and despair by distorting God's image, motives, or concern. His lies convince us that God doesn't love us or care about us. The enemy of our souls delights in maximizing our problems and minimizing God's power. Fear distorts how we view crisis, immobilizing us, causing us to dread our future; this, too, is a type of doubt. Sometimes the crisis distorts our view of who God is; he appears smaller while our problems are super-sized, enlarged to gigantic and exaggerated proportions. Perhaps the optical illusion is upsizing our fears and doubts. That can be paralyzing. Have you ever felt like you were uncomfortably rigid, that you wanted to move forward but were unable to? I can relate.

Prayer in fear

Moving forward after Paul's death, I needed to be strong. I wanted to have courage, but I felt so weak and frightened. Then I remembered a prayer Beth Moore had taught us at a women's conference, a prayer she prayed for her family. I had prayed the same prayer for my family for about six weeks: "Lord, protect my family from everything but your glory." I had to choose how I would walk through the valley of the shadow of death. I decided that Paul's death would magnify God's power. I prayed this prayer in faith, that God would use this time for his glory and that, as I asked despite my fear, according to God's will, it would come to pass. "Lord, protect my family from everything but God's glory." I—wondered—would this phrase ring true in the unknown future? I told God I wasn't sure about that, but in faith I prayed the prayer. God could be trusted with my honesty and my feelings.

Honesty policy

God wants us to be honest, even in doubt, anger, fear, and bitterness. Openness and vulnerability are difficult, aren't they? Both are scary and almost impossible, especially if we are mad at God. Doubt is a close relative of fear. We must make up our minds to believe. We must decide we are going to trust God, stand firm, and remain steadfast in our faith. In scripture, God used Abram to show us how to set aside fear and step out in faith. Abram's story begins when God calls him into ministry in Genesis 12:1, 4: "The Lord had said to Abram, 'Go from your country, your people and your father's household to the land I will show you.'… So, Abram went, as the Lord had told him; and Lot went with him." Abram made his mind up to believe, and that, too, was the decision I made. I would believe God and anticipate the future with hope.

The only information Abram had to go on was God's promise to guide and bless him. His decision to follow God set into motion the development of the nation of Israel, preparing the way for the coming of Jesus Christ. God works in our lives through faith, not unbelief. It's so important for us to understand this because we don't want to live in situations where God won't do anything because of our unbelief.[2]

God wants us to come to him dependently, with naked, emotional honesty, confessing our lack of faith, our failure, and yes, even our fears. If we yearn to have a strong faith in God, we will certainly wrestle with doubt and unbelief. We must choose to trust God. Even in doubt, we must choose to walk forward in faith, despite how we feel about our situation. We might find ourselves in a place we question him. We are uncertain and confused. It is in this very position we are forced to recognize our inadequacy, inability, and lack of faith, even while we remain receptive to God's activity. "Faith does not operate in the realm of the possible. There is no glory for God in that which is humanly possible. Faith begins where man's power ends." George Mueller[3]

Abram didn't understand how his position as "the father of nations" would happen. He struggled as he attempted to do what God told him to do. He had major issues with fear along the way. Abram and his group traveled through Egypt, and when the Egyptians saw Sarah, they were amazed at her beauty. They insisted on taking her to their Pharaoh to show her off. Fear gripped Abram so much that he didn't trust God with his and Sarah's protection. Abram was deceived and worried about his safety. He feared if the Egyptians knew he was Sarah's husband, they would kill him so Pharaoh could add her to his harem. Abram told her to lie. "Say you are my sister, so that I will be treated well for your sake and my life will be spared because of you" (Genesis 12:13). Abram was fearful; he wavered in his faith, but God protected him and his family. It's remarkable how God can even use liars and the fearful; can you relate?

A time to grieve

In the days, weeks, and months after Paul's death, I faced my fears of a life without a partner. *It isn't fair*, I thought. I liked being married; I enjoyed my role as a pastor's wife. Now

I was single and alone, and everything about my daily life was much more difficult. Especially challenging was the area of my finances because there was now only one income. I took each day one at a time, trying not to get ahead of God's leading. Like Abram, I "set out and didn't know where I was going," but I kept moving forward. I made plans to find answers, truth, and hope by staying connected with God and his people. I had made up my mind to believe and to trust that God would protect me. That was not always easy for Abram to do, and it was not always easy for me. How about for you?

My journey through grief often clouded my view of God, making him appear distorted, like in a house of mirrors; he seemed much smaller than my looming loss. I was challenged to wonder if his character truly was reliable. I chose to keep going, putting one foot in front of the other, and move on. Attending my church's GriefShare group and weekly counseling in Norm's office, I learned how to wade through the valley of the shadow of death. I felt very "in the dark" about so many things concerning my loss but discovered that God saw everything going on. I was so relieved once I understood that I didn't need to explain anything to God. As a widow, no one really knew my daily schedule, and now there was no one with whom to share the daily chores, bills, and responsibilities, but I became more and more confident of God's faithful presence. "Even the darkness will not be dark to you; the night will shine like the day, for darkness is as light to you" (Psalm 139:12).

It was hard for me to trust people with emotions about my loss, but I knew those in my support group were safe. We shared the common bond of losing a loved one; we were members of the same club, one none of us had wanted to join. The GriefShare videos brought encouragement. We heard testimonies of others who had lost their spouses, pushing through life alone, people who could understand secondary losses. The term "secondary losses" was a new one to me. Not only had I lost a spouse, but I'd also lost the roles I depended on my husband to fill: friend, handyman, lover, gardener, companion, provider, ministry partner, mentor, prayer partner, source of my inspiration, father to our children, counselor, couple's friend, couple's class, pastor. In identifying each one of these secondary losses and grieving them individually, I learned to relinquish my expectations and rights for Paul to be there for me. I mourned every loss. I received comfort and peace as a result of letting go of Paul—after all, he wasn't mine. "Yes my soul, find rest in God; my hope comes from him. Truly he is my rock and my salvation; he is my fortress, I will not be shaken" (Psalm 62:5-6).

You may not have lost a loved one, but has your secondary loss come with the loss of freedom or mobility because of an illness? Or possibly the loss of friends and church with a move? Or have you had a recent loss of income with a demotion or layoff in your employment? Maybe you are now an empty nester, or an adult child has recently married and you are letting go of parenting him or her. Perhaps you've been incarcerated for several years, and a decade or two have slipped by as you have been behind bars. Whatever primary and secondary losses you have endured, be sure that God knows, God cares, and he will restore to you what you have lost. Joel 2:25 states, "I will repay you for the years the locusts have eaten."

I discovered how to express my feelings in my daily quiet times alone with God; it helped immensely to write them down. I knew I couldn't trust my feelings. I recalled during my battle with cancer, before the nurses hooked up my IV for the chemo sessions, they would ask where on a scale of one to ten, if I was experiencing any pain. In the same way, the journal provided by GriefShare asked, "Describe the level of your pain as it is today." I found great resolve as I sorted, named, and wrote down every unraveled and raw feeling. I chose to not bury my pain; I felt lighter as the words filled up page after page and freed my emotions. As a wonderful added bonus, I could usually find an encouraging scripture typed into the text of the journal, scripture that helped soothe my spirit's soreness and bind up my broken heart. Here's one example: "Very truly I tell you, you will weep and mourn while the world rejoices. You will grieve, but your grief will turn to joy... Now is your time of grief, but I will see you again and you will rejoice, and no one will take away your joy" (John 16:20, 22). Week after week as I went to counseling and attended the classes, I began to accept God's comfort and better understand the differences in the ways my family and I grieved. I found creative ways to help my family in their grief, accepted support from others, and started to think again about my own identity.

These same principles apply to any loss, including those mentioned above: If we let him God will help us to move forward. God sees all we are going through in a dark time, for me, for Abram, and for you too. God discussed his promise with Abram in Genesis 15: 1, 5: "After this, the word of the LORD came to Abram in a vision: 'Do not be afraid, Abram.

I am your shield, your very great reward.'... He took him out-side and said, 'Look up at the sky and count the stars—if in-deed you can count them.' Then he said to him, 'So shall your offspring be.'" Just as God showed Abram the truth of his fu-ture when he told him to look up at the light of the numer-ous stars, we too can be encouraged as the light of God's truth pushes through our dark clouds of doubt and fear.

I learned I had a choice about how I would grieve. It was up to me to work through my grief, and if I did, it would take me to a place of compassion for others. I knew grievers who seemed stuck in selfishly running "awful-izing circles" around their own losses. I didn't judge them but noticed they weren't moving through their grief—they remained stuck. Awful-izing circles convince us that our situation is worse than anyone else's and that God doesn't care about us. Even in grief and loss, we must understand that this type of doubt can move us toward unbelief. We can move closer to God and dig deeper into our faith if we focus on the truth.

The truth is, "You and I will be different because of our grief," as H. Norman Wright says in his booklet *Experiencing Grief.*[4] I wanted my grief to change me, draw me closer to God, allow me to be different, to grow, and did not want to waste the pain of the nearly unbearable grief of losing Paul. I chose to put effort into moving through my grief. Well-mean-ing friends, attempting to encourage me, shared advice and made comments about how I should be doing, "You should be over Paul by now." Although I wanted to snap back, *I will never be over Paul*, I calmly answered, "I will let you know what I need." Maybe you, too, had to hold your tongue when others tried to encourage you but their words seemed to make things worse? Have you ever had to think fast before you came up with a gentle answer to those who want to help, but weren't? I can relate.

Unknown territory

Like Abram, and maybe you, I was most afraid of the unknown future. How would I make ends meet, and what would come next? I was especially encouraged and surprised by the greater awareness I experienced at how my different losses affected me. I *chose* not to let grief cloud my eyes to the fact that God is good and has a plan for eternity. I learned that in order to receive God's comfort, I needed to place myself where his comfort is. I preferred spending time in prayer, reading the Bible, being with other believers and family members, and listening to Christian music. It was amazing, as I sought God's comfort, how he came through again. Through his people, those who understood and prayed with me, he provided abundant peace and hope.

My broken heart began to be put back together, one small piece at a time. "The Lord is close to the brokenhearted and saves those who are crushed in spirit" (Psalm 34:18). And then my faith began to grow. Instead of feeling overcome with sadness when I thought about Paul, my memories comforted me. Sometimes I laughed when I remembered a few of the crazy things we had done while dating. I no longer began crying because of my loss when I recalled the happy times—the births of our children, wedding anniversaries, birthday parties, and family gatherings. Remembering these instances now helped my gloom to lift. When we choose to accept losses of any kind, through choosing belief and push through them instead of turning over to doubt, growth takes place. What losses are you facing? Will you allow God to turn them into growth?

Against all hope

After the Lord told Abram what was coming, he believed in God. But there is a difference in believing in God and believing God will come through. God laid out his covenant promise and, as a reminder, changed Abram's name to Abraham in Genesis 17:5: "No longer will you be called Abram; your name will be called Abraham, for I have made you a father of many nations." It didn't seem humanly possible that God would enable Abraham to be the father of nations. There was no physical reason to believe Abraham and Sarah would have a child. They needed a miracle. Romans 4:18-21 tells us, "Against all hope, Abraham in hope believed and so became the father of many nations, just as it had been said to him, 'So shall your offspring be.' Without weakening in his faith, he faced the fact that his body was as good as dead—since he was about a hundred years old—and that Sarah's womb was also dead. Yet he did not waver through unbelief regarding the promise of God, but was strengthened in his faith and gave glory to God, being fully persuaded that God had power to do what he had promised."

We, today, continue to reap the long-term effects of Abraham's faithfulness. We learn how Abraham conquered his fears by depending on God, and depending on God once led to his being able to depend on him again, which is one thing we are learning in those dark valleys. Abraham didn't rely on his ability to please God, but on God's freely given provision as Almighty God. "Abram believed the Lord, and he credited it to him as righteousness" (Genesis 15:6).

As I dug into my life without a husband, some days it seemed like I barely survived, but it didn't take too long before I began to relish my singleness. I found a new beginning amid my losses, and instead of being afraid of the fresh start, I embraced the sudden adventure. This would not have been possible if I had continued reacting in fear or panic. I'd figured out that my root fear was going through life alone, and as God's presence became more real to me, I knew I didn't have to fly solo. God was there. That was the key. Once I figured out what had caused me to be afraid, I could stay focused on the truth. Isaiah 54:4-5a (NIV) says, "Do not be afraid; you will not be put to shame. Do not fear disgrace; you will not be humiliated. You will forget the shame of your youth and remember no more the reproach of your widowhood. For your Maker is your husband"—I didn't have to be concerned; I could count on God to be my husband.

Take away

Instead of living in fear and being overwhelmed by circumstances from the past or present, we must remember, "Life's events don't determine who we are or what we feel—it is our perception of those events. If what we believe does not reflect the truth, then what we feel will not reflect reality."[5] We can't control our emotions, but we can control what we choose to think. What we choose to think affects what we believe. If what we believe does not reflect the truth, then what we feel will not

91

reflect reality. Fear can be changed to faith as we allow truth to take hold of our anxiety. We must choose to believe truth to feel better. "For though we live in the world, we do not wage war as the world does. The weapons we fight with are not the weapons of the world. On the contrary, they have divine power to demolish strongholds. We demolish arguments and every pretension that sets itself up against the knowledge of God, and we take captive every thought to make it obedient to Christ" (2 Corinthians 10:3-5).

Mended and whole

Sometimes my feelings told me, "You will never feel good again." I held on to what I knew to be true: "The Lord is close to the brokenhearted; he rescues those whose spirits are crushed" (Psalm 34:18, NLT). This verse had new meaning to me. I had invited God into my waiting room. We will explore the waiting room concept together in Chapter 8, but essentially, the phrase means "waiting for God's timing to reveal his will." When we invite God to be part of whatever or whomever we are waiting on, the light of his word counters our fears, doubts, and impatience. I confess, I had been holding God's plans for me at a distance. I was so tired and didn't think I had the energy to ask his forgiveness, but I knew he wanted me to humble myself and ask forgiveness for doing things my way. I knew the next step was to allow God to help me forgive those who had hurt our family by not walking with us during our time of grief. My unmet expectations of who I thought should care for my children and me were causing me anguish. Each week as I visited Norm's office, he would mention, "Sheryl it is time to let go of your anger." I wasn't ready. And so I procrastinated in letting go of my expectations, hurt, and pain. Deep down, I thought people might think I had loved Paul less if I moved on. The opposite is true—to move forward in a healthy way means you had a positive experience at the time and you are now willing to continue growing.

We are no longer helpless in our struggle to decide whether to go God's way or our own way. We can choose to lean on God's understanding by determining he will win. Our minds can be truly free as they are renewed, transformed, and healed by that faith. We have the freedom to choose: we can keep our minds set on God's goodness and the great things he has done, not on our problems. Truth soothes our fears, changes our feelings, and shapes our thoughts. The truth is what we most need when we are hurt the deepest.

Where can you find that truth? Absolute truth and the right words for you to pray are found in God's word. When you spend time in it, you will see God as he is, not as Satan would like you to see him, with his attitude as uncaring and his power as distorted as those funhouse mirrors. Psalm 119:28-30 says, "My soul is weary with sorrow; strengthen me according to your word. Keep me from deceitful ways; be gracious to me and teach me your law. I have chosen the way of faithfulness; I have set my heart on your laws." You and I, like Abraham, have a choice to keep our mind set to walk forward by faith, eagerly anticipating that God has something good in store. Don't overthink your problems. Don't keep trying to do something you can't do, and don't keep trying to figure everything out. Do what you know to do. Let God do the rest.

Can you relate?

Has your view of God become distorted by your anxiety, fears, or loss?

Have you wanted to move forward but are unable to?

Describe your losses: what are you most afraid of?

Commit to go forward.

Chapter 6:

THIS TOO SHALL PASS

"Faith and doubt both are needed – not as antagonists,
but working side by side to take us around the unknown
curve." Lillian Smith[1]

Time magazine's Person of the Year in 2013,
Pope Francis, gave a sincere, candid view of his observations
of doubt. Perhaps, you think this happened in a face-to-face
counseling session with one of his parishioners; on the contrary, the Pope shared his thoughts publicly, during a General
Audience in St. Peter's Square. The doubts were his own—not
from someone he'd been counseling! "Who among us has not
experienced insecurity, loss and even doubts on their journey
of faith? Everyone! We've all experienced this, me too. Everyone. It is part of the journey of faith; it is part of our lives. This
should not surprise us, because we are human beings, marked
by fragility and limitations."[2] The Pope says to expect doubt

on our life's journey. Doubt is part of being human, so when we doubt, we shouldn't feel condemned. He reminded us to do what we already know we should do—not to panic but trust God during difficult times with prayer and find the courage to ask for help. I discovered doubting was easy for me, but asking for help was difficult. Can you remember a time you knew you should ask for help but didn't? Me too.

Tunnel vision

Single again after Paul's death, I kept myself busy but still struggled to make ends meet both emotionally and financially. I worked two jobs, stayed connected with small groups, ministry assignments, and church activities, and attended my weekly counseling sessions with Norm. One night while driving home from an event, I couldn't focus very well on the freeway exit sign in the distance. I couldn't determine how far away the sign was from the front of my car or if it was indeed my exit. I pressed my eyelids close together without closing them all the way, squinting and straining to see in the murky darkness, but doing so did not help at all. I'd hoped that narrowing my eyes would help me focus, but the sign still remained blurred. Alarmed, I kept my attention riveted on the taillights in front of me and tried to stay in between the parallel white lines on the freeway. This wasn't a complete surprise; my night vision had been partially challenged for at least six months, so I had avoided driving after dark.

That night our small group had gone overtime. It was a few hours past sunset; the evening sky was now completely black. I'd had no other option—I had to drive myself home. I wondered, *What is wrong with my eyesight?* Earlier in the week, my sight had seemed blurry in the day too. I'd cleaned my contact lenses thoroughly, put the right lens in the right eye, blinked in an attempt to focus, but my view was still clouded. So I'd popped the contact lens out and put on my farsighted glasses, instead. I wore them nearly all the time.

After small group, while trying to get my freeway bearings, I tilted my eyeglasses up a bit to get a better view but had no success. Even with my farsighted lenses on, my vision was blurred and cloudy, like looking through a foggy window. No amount of contorting, squinting, or adjusting helped me see better, and I swerved a little too close to another vehicle, nearly broadsiding them. I pulled my car off to the side of the road to gain my composure. *Whew, that was close. That's it,* I decided, *no more delays or excuses.* I would make an appointment to get my eyesight checked the next day. Shadows of doubt loomed, and I wondered if the cancer had returned. I wanted and needed to know what was wrong; I had put it off long enough. I was in denial about having a problem, and I couldn't ignore it any longer. After an appointment with my optometrist, I was diagnosed with cataracts. I received treatment to remedy the problem soon after the diagnosis. It was wonderful to see clearly once again. Maybe you, too, have postponed and regretted giving attention to an important health need. If we knew the consequences, what might we have done differently?

The smokescreen of procrastination

Procrastination is a close relative of fear. We don't doubt that God is able to do what we need him to do for us. But we

97

wonder, *Will God do it for me?* We don't want to begin, because we don't want to fail or face the truth of what we believe is just ahead. So we make excuses, set unreasonable target dates, and self-sabotage to ensure we don't gain momentum. God wants us not to doubt ourselves or him; he wants us to stop examining and retrying our failed solutions and our ways of solving things and instead trust him. He wants us not to get sucked into the paralysis of analysis, but he encourages us to step into our future by faith.

Some of us run away from dealing with situations because of fear. Fear is an emotional response to an unknown future or uncomfortable situation. Fear can motivate us to faith. But fear can also cause us to doubt God and his provision, opening the door for defense mechanisms such as self-pity, discouragement, anger, depression, and even procrastination. The Hebrew word for fear is *pachad*,[3] meaning to tremble, to be in trepidation, to be on one's guard, or to have terror. Each of these definitions can relate to the daily and often harsh circumstances of life, ultimately causing us to be fearful.

Often, because we are afraid, we postpone doing what needs to be done, putting it off until a better time, a time which never comes. Here's the definition of procrastinate (transitive verb): to put off intentionally and habitually; (intransitive verb): to put off intentionally the doing of something that should be done. [4] A key element in overcoming fear and procrastination is the decision to let God lead. And then we immediately follow him, rather than doing the equivalent of holding off, squinting, or cleaning our glasses, hoping the problem will go away on its own. Once we are moving, stepping forward by faith, we enter our destiny. Procrastination limits our faith vision because we choose to see only what is in that limited, sometimes blurry area. Objects such as God's love and provision are not very clear. Shapes, such as people who care or want to encourage, are there, but the clarity of what they represent cannot be seen. We might mistrust them or their motives. We recognize the outline or the colors or the shape, but we cannot see the details.

In my grief, God provided people who entered my journey, burden-bearers who walked along with me. Instead of focusing on them, I was angry and sad about those who chose not to be involved in our lives. When I got to a place in my journey where I knew the final step was to let go of my anger, I knew I must not procrastinate. I had to let my anger go. This procedure applies to any situation where God shines his light of truth, whether it be letting go of doubt through admitting our foiled expectations or releasing dead dreams, frustrated ideas, or unmet goals. If we ask for his help, he will give us what we need to have a proper perspective and will offer solutions to move us forward into renewed hope.

Jesus came to make us free through the truth. "And you shall know the truth, and the truth shall make you free" (John 8:32, NKJV). We can build up our relationship with God in difficult circumstances if we choose to live close to God. This choice allows us to face our fears and the truth about ourselves. Instead of staying stuck in procrastination, we can anticipate progress. We must start by looking into the mirror of God's word—we read the word, and the word reads us—and we then see ourselves the way God sees us, as well as seeing God clearly.

We can see the best way forward, even if it's something we don't want to do: forgive those who have hurt us.

I'll forgive it…tomorrow

"You need to get rid of your anger, hurt, and hate," my grief counselor, Norm, repeated. I'd become very irritated with Norm's insistence week after week about what I needed to do. And now it felt like he was nagging and meddling in my business. *Who is he to tell me how to run my life?* Because of my years of sitting on the client side of the counseling desk and my familiarity with the reverse of that on the lay-counselor side, I knew it was highly unusual for a counselor to give advice. But I knew he was right.

My old adversary, doubt, haunted me for months as I put off forgiving my offenders for not caring enough and as I procrastinated dealing with and getting rid of my hurt and hate toward them. *They don't deserve to be forgiven* was one excuse for my very long list of wrongs my offenders had committed against our family. I wanted to nurse my wounds, rehearse my pain, and curse these offenders as long as possible. I thought if I could keep reviewing the ways they hurt my family and me, it would hurt them. Little did I know this was one of the reasons I had trouble sleeping. I knew what God's word said: "Instead, be kind to each other, tenderhearted, forgiving one another, just as God has forgiven you because you belong to Christ" (Ephesians 4:32, TLB). I wasn't sure if this would work for me. My anger was still strong.

My deceased husband Paul's vivacious ministry spanned more than thirty years and three congregations, serving people from the cradle to the grave. It seemed as if those who left me and my children alone in our grief didn't care about us. It felt like they discounted and minimized Paul's life influence and the eternal impact he had on the discipleship journey of scores of believers. You, too, might feel abandoned by people or by God, the result of past church experience, a divorce, a job loss, or anything else when your circumstances pushed you into a place you would rather not be.

The only way I could receive the emotional healing I so desperately needed was to get rid of my resentment—God's way. The offense of unforgiveness kept me in chains; I was beginning to understand how bad the toxic emotion of bitterness had been, blocking me from others through isolation and pride. I didn't want to forgive them, but I knew God commanded it. "But when you are praying, first forgive anyone you are holding a grudge against, so that your Father in heaven will forgive you your sins too" (Mark 11:25, TLB). I've learned there is a lot of confusion about what forgiveness looks like. It's not denying that something happened or necessarily trusting that person again (though it can be). Forgiveness is a choice, a decision, a crisis of the will. Forgiveness is not forgetting, but it is agreeing to live with the consequences of another person's sin and choosing not to hold that person's sin against him or her anymore. When God says he "remembers your sins no more" (Isaiah 43:25), this means he will not use our past against us. Forgetting might be a result of forgiveness, but it is not a means toward it. The Holy

Spirit, again, was standing next to the closet door, waiting to open it, so that he and I could clean it out together. It was time.

Jonah's journey

"First-time obedience. Delayed obedience is disobedience." These were two of the principles suggested in the parenting classes Paul and I had attended many years earlier to find out to learn how to better parent our young children. These concepts were refreshing and gave us hope during the formative years as we helped our kids learn how to follow through. The specific guidelines sounded tangible and practical, but we wondered if the skills were transferable to our children. We were used to asking our children to do their chores, but they did not immediately jump up to fulfill our command. I realized I don't always immediately jump up and do what God asks me to do, such as forgiving those who had hurt my children and me by their benign neglect. I needed to ensure I was not delaying obedience. A beloved Bible character struggled with that too. Not only did Jonah disobey God, but he also took matters into his own hands when God told him to preach to Nineveh.

"Jonah was a devoted countryman who had an allegiance to his country. He had a deep love for his people and wanted the Israelites to continue to flourish and their enemies to flounder."[5] Jonah had grown up hating the Assyrians and fearing their atrocities. The Assyrians were guilty of evil plots against God, exploitation of the helpless, cruelty in war, idolatry, prostitution, and witchcraft. Jonah despised the Assyrians so much he didn't want them to receive God's mercy—he wanted them to perish for their crimes. Jonah tried to make sense of God's instructions to preach to those Assyrians, but he just couldn't bring himself to follow through. He didn't understand or agree with God's love for the Assyrians. Jonah not only postponed his obedience to God, but also was flat-out disobedient. Jonah 1:3 tells us, "But Jonah ran away from the LORD and headed for Tarshish. He went down to Joppa, where he found a ship bound for that port. After paying the fare, he went aboard and sailed for Tarshish to flee from the LORD." Now, I'm not saying that those who had hurt me had sinned against me or hurt me to this level. But they had hurt me, even if not purposely I needed to push past that, and I did. God in his grace allowed me time to heal to the point I could respond with forgiveness.

Delayed obedience

I had put it off long enough; I knew what to do. I was done procrastinating—it was time for me to forgive. I had offered forgiveness in the past, and it had been freeing to let go of those hurts, habits, and hang-ups. I had come to grips with the truth that forgiveness is a choice, a decision, a crisis of the will. Jesus reminds us in Luke 6:36, "Be merciful, just as your Father is merciful." God has shown us mercy that we don't deserve. I experienced firsthand how it works: we show mercy through forgiveness, and that is a way to keep the lines of communication open between God and us. When we forgive someone who doesn't deserve to be forgiven, we are giving up our right to get even and letting go of taking our own revenge. God will deal with them, and we can trust that God will judge them in his way and his time. God is a righteous judge, who reminds us in Romans 12:19, " 'It is mine to avenge, I will repay,' says the Lord." When we take people off our "hook," we can be sure they are never off God's "hook."

We are told we must forgive "so that no advantage is taken of us by Satan, for we are not ignorant of his schemes" (2 Corinthians 2:11, NASB). It was up to me. I had to choose to forgive my offenders, although I thought they didn't deserve it. 1 Corinthians 13:5 says that love "keeps no record of wrongs." This scripture reminded me that love, God's love, doesn't keep lists of anything or anyone that has hurt, angered, offended, or wronged us. One of the most difficult steps of faith is to release the offenses we have suffered into the hands of God. "'Look, the Lamb of God, who takes away the sin of the world," (John 1:29). Jesus's crucifixion wounds rightfully belonged to us; he was punished in our place to satisfy God's sacrificial requirement. His sacrifice provided for our righteousness. "Christ had no sin, but God made him become sin so that in Christ we could become right with God" (2 Corinthians 5:21, ERV).

No regret

Martin Luther King Jr. said, "Forgiveness is not an occasional act, but a permanent attitude." Remember Jesus's dying words from Luke 23:34: "Father, forgive them, for they do not know what they are doing." Forgiveness is a supernatural act, yet it is essential to our faith. Ask God to help you. "Be gentle and ready to forgive; never hold grudges. Remember, the Lord forgave you, so you must forgive others" (Colossians 3:13, TLB).

My desire is for you and me to learn to live with no regrets. One of the biggest regrets I have about wading through that time of grief was how I put off, procrastinated, getting rid of the hurt and hate toward my offenders. Your responses to this resource might vary, but this is a template for you to follow if you choose. I didn't feel it was the Lord's timing for me to contact those I forgave, although for some, that might be part of what God asks you to do. Remember, choosing to forgive is an act of obedience for you, and it is between you and God, not between you and your offender.

I learned a few profound truths about how to offer forgiveness, along with a simple prayer to forgive my offenders. I sat down and listed the names of people who had caused me pain. As I remembered what they did or didn't do for me, I wrote down how that had made me feel. Neil T. Anderson says, "If your forgiveness doesn't touch the emotional core of your life, it will be incomplete."[6] The prayer I used is specific. Fill in the person's name in the first blank and how he made you feel in the second blank. For every memory, no matter how painful, say aloud the name and the feelings associated with each person on the list.

"Dear Lord Jesus, I choose to forgive (name the person) for (what he or she did or failed to do), because it made me feel (share the painful feelings—rejected, dirty, worthless, inferior, etc.)."

After you have forgiven every person for every painful memory, pray as follows:

"Lord Jesus, I choose not to hold on to my resentment. I relinquish my right to seek revenge and ask you to heal my damaged emotions. Thank you for setting me free from the bondage of my bitterness. I now ask you to bless those who have hurt me. In Jesus's name I pray. Amen."[7]

Have you been waiting on the right time to deal with something—perhaps forgiveness, perhaps something else? You will never feel like taking care of it, but you must act anyway. Why don't you take a few moments right now to deal with any bitterness and anger toward those who have hurt you? You will be glad you did.

Longing to be sure

Doubt by procrastination is putting off a decision or postponing facing a problem, which leads to consequences that can be avoided if we face the issue a little earlier than we'd planned. I would have released my bitterness, slept better, and been happier if I'd obeyed sooner. Why hadn't I? I didn't think my offenders deserved my forgiveness. This is how Jonah refused to obey. He did not agree with God nor want him to have mercy on the Ninevites. He ran away from the Lord, heading in the opposite direction. When a terrible storm threatened the ship full of unaware sailors, Jonah knew why—it was his fault because of his disobedience. Finally, disobedience was painful enough that Jonah was ready to own up to the situation and suffer the consequences. Jonah 1:9-15 (TLB) recounts, "Then he told them he was running away from the Lord. The men were terribly frightened when they heard this. 'Oh, why did you do it?' they shouted. 'What should we do to you to stop the storm?' For it was getting worse and worse. 'Throw me out into the sea,' he said, 'and it will become calm again. For I know this terrible storm has come because of me.' They tried harder to row the boat ashore, but couldn't make it. The storm was too fierce to fight against. Then they shouted out a prayer to Jehovah, Jonah's God. 'O Jehovah,' they pleaded, 'don't make us die for this man's sin, and don't hold us responsible for his death, for it is not our fault—you have sent this storm upon him for your own good reasons. ' Then they picked up Jonah and threw him overboard into the raging sea—and the storm stopped! "

Jonah had lots of time to think about his decisions and was convicted during his time in the belly of the whale. Finally, God got his attention and was able to move Jonah to the direction God had planned all along.

Essential doubt

There is a difference between unbelief and doubt. Doubt is when we have experienced a roadblock to a more solid faith or deeper relationship with God. Doubt is not unbelief. Pope Francis confirms that doubt is an essential part of our faith. "If one has the answers to all the questions—that is the proof that God is not with him. It means that he is a false prophet using religion for himself. The great leaders of the people of God, like Moses, have always left room for doubt. You must leave room for the Lord, not for our certainties; we must be humble."[8]

As we learned previously, unbelief is the decision to live your life as if there is no God. On the contrary, doubt is a longing to be sure of what or whom we trust. When we move from doubt to deeper faith by choosing belief, we must let go of our unrealistic ideas about faith. When doubt is answered by trust, and faith is fed, doubt becomes belief. Starve your doubts, feed your faith. We can be confident of victory if we put our trust and confidence only in God and not in ourselves.

Do it now

God's discipline focused on the care of his prophet and the people he wanted to reach through him; God's discipline in my life was no different. God got my attention as I was in the depths of my grief journey. No matter what your journey is—loss, disappointment, failure, tragedy—if God has spoken to you about the subject of forgiveness, maybe it is time for you to stop procrastinating. Like Jonah, I did not want God to have mercy on my offenders. *After all, they were church people, and they should have known better,* I thought. As I forgave them, even though I felt they didn't deserve to be forgiven, I was freed; I could see clearly once more. God wanted me to let go not only for their good but also for my good. Won't you choose to forgive your offenders, even if you feel they don't deserve it?

Can you relate?

Have you postponed forgiving someone?

Describe your "delayed obedience."

Are you ready to put aside your fears and make plans to face the truth?

Share what you anticipate will be different once you follow through.

Chapter 7:

SECOND CHANCE

"We are mirrors whose brightness is wholly derived from
the sun that shines upon us."
C. S. Lewis[1]

The Yellowstone fires [2] *burned* uncontrollably
from mid-June until the first snow in September 1988. Rav-
enous and frenzied fires wiped out 1.2 million acres, affecting
about 36 percent of the park's over two-million acres of lush
sequoia forest. As the damage was tallied, it became clear that
the financial losses could not be recovered. Incredibly, years after the Yellowstone fires, the sequoias actually increased in pro-
ductivity. After the fires, the wooded area was more open; more
light reached the forest floor. Where the fire had burned hottest
was an ideal seedbed for the giant sequoia seedlings. The heat
of the fire caused the sequoia cones to open and thousands of
seeds to release and fall to the soil.

Even though we may have had a personal devastation, a fire which burned us in some way, the same type of mental, spiritual, and emotional restoration is available for you and me. With our cooperation, God can use any loss to make us healthier than ever. Though we might feel like our pain will never end, God has a divine plan; as we submit to that plan, we allow his gentle healing to take place in his way and his time. He will restore, rebuild, and regenerate our lives. God wants to restore our broken relationships, transform us more into the image of Christ, and he wants to bring us closer to the complete, satisfying wholeness God has for us. Why? It's all about him. I knew this truth and was happy to share it with others, but when it came to applying it to the smoldering embers of my losses, I struggled.

Renewed resolve

I hadn't wanted my former life to go up in flames; nevertheless, it did. I was surrounded by the charred residue, the ashes of disappointment, discouragement, and despair. Unnerving questions came to my mind in droves, usually keeping me awake at night, this insomnia worse than the side effects of taking steroids during chemo. I knew my crazy feelings of grief and deep sorrow were normal. It felt good to cry and let my tears offer some relief, yet I wanted the hurt of being human to be erased. I was tired—tired of grieving and tired of trying to figure out what was next.

I didn't want to let go of the future I had planned, yet God was asking me to relinquish my agenda, plans, and goals. The doubt that surfaced this time was new: I doubted that the life

I was now to embrace would be better than the life I'd had before. I thought there was nothing good ahead in this new life I had not planned. Tentatively, I let go of my expectations—life as I thought it would be—and decided to embrace my new normal.

It took time, but gradually, as I kept up with my healing journey, I began to feel more and more confident, sure of myself, able to push through and make important decisions on my own. God encouraged me with a second chance. As a single woman, I'd humbled myself in my financial struggles, making major decisions, such as buying a car, putting a new roof on my home, remodeling a bathroom, traveling to Africa alone, and even changing jobs. That humility and action brought surprising confidence that led to new opportunities.

Surprised by ministry

I felt empowered; I was given amazing opportunities to share hope and healing with individuals and groups in my local community and eventually overseas. I shared about the renewal God had given me in grief and loss, one-on-one with my new friends, support groups, and counseling sessions. My children healed and matured too. I was surprised one day, several months before my son's graduation from college, when he asked, "Mom, what do you need from me?" I thought he might be inquiring about the need for some maintenance projects or sorting through the garage in our family home. But I knew those projects could wait. I thought about what I needed from him and what he needed from me and felt it was a critical time for us to travel together, as mother and son, so that I could introduce him to his father's and my friends in Africa. So about nine months after Paul's passing, we spent time in Kenya, the Democratic Republic of the Congo, and Egypt visiting dear ministry partners, with a bonus of many chances to minister to widows, orphans, pastors, and seminary students. The time was valuable for my son, but also a refining time for me to evaluate my path forward and hear from God about what was next. God had a good plan for my future.

Little did I know this would be the first of my many treks to Africa. Each time I obediently made the time-consuming, financially draining, and physically taxing trip, God graciously stitched together another piece of my broken heart. He used the love of my overseas friends to renew me, and he used my obedience to minister to others and build them up. Each trip overseas was serendipitous. I thought I might, in a remote way, encourage these dear saints, but I found their love and hospitality was, instead, a gift to me—one I happily received! God gave me a second chance by allowing me to trust him with my future and enlarged my heart to care about others in ways I hadn't expected. Psalm 18:19 says, "He brought me out to a spacious place; he rescued me because he delighted in me." I wonder if you are facing a life adjustment you'd rather not? Surprisingly good things lie ahead!

Priestly prayer

A familiar Bible character, Zechariah, gives insight on how to face impossible life changes. A devoted Levite priest reputed as "upright to God," Zechariah and his wife were unable to conceive. Their barrenness was a curse and certainly not the life they had planned. Yet these two remained faithful to God. During a regular prayer offering, the angel of the Lord appeared to Zechariah, startling him to attention with the announcement that a son would be born to his wife, Elizabeth. Zechariah skeptically answered, "How can I be sure of this? I am an old man and my wife is well along in years" (Luke 1:18.) From a human perspective, Zechariah's doubts were understandable; after all, the couple were way past the age of childbearing. It can be simple to doubt or misunderstand what God wants to do in our lives, especially if we've grown used to trusting our own intellect or personal experiences. His power, however, is shown in our weakness and our decision to depend on God. When we are tempted to think that one of God's promises is impossible, we must remind ourselves of his work throughout history. Nothing is impossible with God. His power is not confined to a narrow perspective or human limitations. We can trust him completely.

Zechariah doubted the possibility of his wife birthing a child. Lack of faith in God's plan didn't prevent God's plan. God is always good, and God always does what is right, even when we doubt he can or will. Rachel Held Evans calls this the "math of doubt." Is doubt a good thing? Well, it is certainly not God's ideal. However, the consistent theme throughout scripture is that God can work with people in the midst of their doubts. Doubt is not a deal breaker. We tend to think that a little bit of doubt can erase a lot of faith. That's not how the math of faith and doubt works. The math of faith and doubt goes like this: A little faith > a lot of doubt. Doubt does not necessarily cancel faith. There may be a time when doubt will hold us back from God, but there is a process and a tension to faith and doubt."[3]

I, and Zechariah, doubted that God had good planned for a future we did not see. No matter our losses or challenges, our doubts about God bringing around a good future must be addressed. We must decide to give God a second chance when presented with a path we haven't asked for and circumstances we didn't want. As we journey forward, turning to God and his word, we will find peace and, in time, the answers we seek.

Identity matters

Especially in times of grief, loss, or a new normal, it is enticing to want to do things our own way. I didn't want to let God remake my future, but with Paul's death, I had to choose to do it his way or my way. Maybe you haven't lost a loved one by death, but your dream has died, or you are sick, or you've moved or lost your job, spouse, or church. You know it's a choice we all must make: we can submit to God and let his peace overrule our fears, procrastination, doubt, or unbelief. As we dig into a deeper faith, pushing away the clouds of skepticism and seeing him the way he really is, we can experience him as the God of second chances.

I went back to what I knew God's word said about me, and I reviewed my identity in Christ, which trumped all the other roles I had been playing.

Early on in my recovery from drugs and alcohol, I decided to let God remake my identity in Christ, to trust him with the results. I experienced firsthand that life doesn't work when something is broken. I learned that God's specialty is taking away our "ashes"—losses, disappointments, despair, and dismay. I came across Isaiah 61:3 at a time when I didn't think I had anything to offer anyone in ministry. It says, "to bestow on them a crown of beauty instead of ashes, the oil of joy instead of mourning, and a garment of praise instead of a spirit of despair." I looked over the verses in Isaiah 61 and was struck by the truth that God can remake our ashes into beauty if we are willing to let him do what he does best: renew.

New normal

After a situation causes us to doubt, as we choose to move forward in new circumstances and faith, we reach a new normal. Each day I would arise early for my time alone with God; it had once seemed like a chore on my "to-do" list. Now, our sweet fellowship became my lifeline. I learned the mere mention of my doubts to God showed him that I admitted there might be a chance he could do something about them—my faith was growing. Daily I dumped my doubts at the feet of God and told him about every one, even though I wasn't sure what would happen next. But I grew certain something good was coming.

In my regular daytime job as the public relations director for a local Christian radio station, my days were filled with meeting with business partners and nonprofit leaders: planning fundraisers and setting up contests; preparing my evening air shift content, and praying with people by phone. I began to heal, slowly, surely, but it took a village to cheer me on. Faithful radio listeners mailed and delivered cards, candy, flowers, and any items they thought might help with my healing. I began to appreciate the soul-mending from grief, and my journey through it was like my recovery from drug and alcohol abuse and even, strangely, like pushing through to my healing from cancer. But I still had to go it alone, and as in my sessions in counseling, it would take intentional, hard work for me to find my "new normal." I knew finding this sweet spot would take time, but I knew it would come. I reached for new dreams and ministries as the light cleared away the fog of doubt. The best was yet to come.

Tell us about it

We all know the result of Zechariah's doubt: through God's gracious correction, he became speechless, and it wasn't because he was in awe of the angel. The angel explained in Luke 1:20 that it was "because you did not believe my words, which will come true at their appointed time." For the duration of his wife Elizabeth's pregnancy, Zechariah was tongue-tied, silent, and unable to communicate with spoken words. The time of being mute was a season of correction for Zechariah. It's wonderful to know that God can use someone, anyone, even while that person is being disciplined. Zechariah learned to listen, to doubt his doubts, and as he did, he was restored.

God in his kindness followed through on his promise and blessed the couple with a son. The time came for Elizabeth and Zechariah to name their son; they had been told what to name him by the angel but had to convince everyone else. Luke 1:63-64 (NIV) describes what happened next: "He asked for a writing tablet, and to everyone's astonishment he wrote, 'His name is John.'" Immediately his mouth was opened and his tongue set free, and he began to speak, praising God."

Zechariah was corrected by God and learned how to trust God in his time of doubt. Do you notice areas you might need to surrender to God? Why not choose to let go? That way God won't have to intervene by tying your tongue, too.

Strange ashes

The Yellowstone fires had at first appeared to be a disaster but were an essential part of the national park's regeneration process. I don't have a green thumb, but I know for new growth to take place that it's necessary to clear out dead wood and excess brush. After the fires, the forest was more open; more light reached the forest floor. Where the fire had been hottest became an ideal seedbed for the seedlings, and, tellingly, the heat of the fire caused giant sequoia cones to open and thousands to be released and fall to the soil. What had been considered a "natural catastrophe" allowed the forest to grow thicker and healthier than before it was burned.

This story reminded me of Isaiah 61:3: "They will be called oaks of righteousness, a planting of the Lord for the display of his splendor." In my losses I knew God had to be growing something bigger and better than I would have planned for myself.

The restoration principle is true for us spiritually too. With our cooperation, God takes the ashes of our losses and, remarkably, uses them as fertilizer to make us spiritually healthier than ever. God offers us second chances and often many more. When we let God transform our losses into something useful, like the fires that burned away the brush blocking the light, and then apply his word with the Holy Spirit as a healing balm, we grow. He doesn't leave us in the fire alone either. "When you pass through the waters, I will be with you; and when you pass through the rivers, they will not sweep over you. When you walk through the fire, you will not be burned; the flames will not set you ablaze" (Isaiah 43:2).

Healthy choices

God's character and nature is always about restoration, renewal, and regeneration. Many of us have watched the television show *Extreme Makeover: Home Edition* and have seen that before a remodel can take place, renovation or demolition must take place first. The Latin term *Capax Dei* means increased capacity for God.[4] Remarkably, this is something you and I can develop by allowing "space" in our lives. When we rid ourselves of doubt, fear, procrastination, bitterness, anger, or any sin that is blocking out the light of the truth, we have made space for healthy growth.

Each of us has a choice. We can let go of that baggage and make room for God to work in our lives. For this to happen, we must make a conscious decision to set aside our doubts and look to God in faith, seeking him in all areas of our lives. We must rid ourselves of thoughts and feelings that weigh us down and replace that void with the truth of God's word.

I invited God to help me rid myself of the things that weighed me down. This happened as I planned times of solitude and silence, and in uninterrupted times with him I intentionally packed up forgiveness, got rid of expectations, and dismissed discouragement. With our cooperation, God will restore, rebuild, and regenerate our life. "You have not given me into the hands of the enemy but have set my feet in a spacious place" (Psalm 31:8). God wants to restore our broken relationships, transform us more into the image of Christ, and bring us closer to the wholeness God has for us. Why? It's all about him.

Fresh start

Maybe you, like Zechariah and me, wonder how things will turn out. When we are surrounded by the ashes of our losses, bitterness, and mistakes, it's difficult to imagine what the new growth will look like or whether it will spring forth as God promises. For months I wasn't sure how, when, or if the pain of grief would end. But soon it didn't matter, with my fresh start, my bright beginning. My new normal became invigorating as I became immersed in ministry, and I was honored when invited to train leaders in Africa and the Middle East. What I had thought was a trip for my son became the foothold to a new ministry. I agree with Robin Jones Gunn, who says, "[When it comes to God] we can't run out of second chances... only time."[5] Because I let go of my expectations, I was able to receive a wonderful gift: I received peace through the evidence of God's love wrapped around my circumstances. "The Lord's unfailing love surrounds the one who trusts in Him" (Psalm 32:10). And this promise gives us great encouragement that with our second chance, it'll be okay. What about you? What new beginning is just ahead for you?

Can you relate?

Describe a time you have felt an extreme loss, then explain how you might see some light come from it.

Share how you experienced a renovation.

Can you relate to Zechariah or me in how you responded?

Relay a time God has renewed or restored a relationship.

Chapter 8

YOU'LL BE FINE

"A soul cannot seek close fellowship with God, or attain
the abiding consciousness of waiting on Him all the day,
without a very honest and entire surrender to all His will."
Andrew Murray[1]

Most of us hate to wait. We can access technology
to avoid waiting; we can order our jeans online to avoid the
agony of long lines; we can ask Google our questions instead
of waiting for an answer from a person; we can even hop on
the internet to schedule dinner reservations to skip waiting for
a seat at our favorite restaurant. We sometimes think of *wait* as
a four-letter word. And it is, of course, but "wait" is *not* a cuss
word. We must wait in a doctor's office or for test results…and
that makes us feel out of control. And we are. But what if our
attitude was adjusted to focus on *how* we wait?

God doesn't move any swifter in the twenty-first century than he did in the first. We can't rush God, but we can allow the time we spend in the "waiting room" to be a time of great personal growth.[2] So we all have a choice: how will we wait? It helps to "invite God into the waiting room." With this step of faith, we are allowing God to have his way and his will while we wait with him, instead of on him. To put it simply, "God's will be done, no matter how long it takes." When we invite God to be part of whatever or whomever we are waiting on, our dark fears, clouded doubts, and gloomy impatience can be countered with the light of his word.

Fully awake

Letting go of my anticipated future with Paul was by far the most difficult thing I had ever done. Nevertheless, I embraced being single, while working two jobs to support myself, and was thrilled to enjoy ample amounts of ministry. In letting go of my expectations, plans, and even my past life, I received much more from God than I expected. I depended on him for everything. He provided for my literal and emotional needs by being closer to me than anyone else. Isaiah 54:5 (NIV) says, "For your Maker is your husband—the Lord Almighty is His name —the Holy One of Israel is your Redeemer; he is called the God of all the earth."

As a single, empty-nester, widowed woman, I felt comfortable making decisions and embracing my new normal. I learned to take care of home repairs, daily chores, ministry obligations, and family commitments. For over twenty-eight years, Paul and I had worked together as a team; I now navigated everything by myself. I made major decisions on my own: purchased a car, arranged a new roof for my home, hired a contractor to remodel a bathroom, changed jobs and even traveled overseas, and accepted invitations to teach at conferences and seminaries in Africa. Yet I anticipated God was preparing me for something more. I was excited and uncertain, a little anxious about what lay ahead. I waited for him to show me what the fulfillment of that anticipation would be. I sensed this was a new stage and that all the work I did by faith and forgiveness was leading to something else, and yet it took time. Might you have experienced these same emotions in a waiting room of your own?

There's more

Most of us wouldn't think of telling God how to bless us. That thought struck me once, when God wanted to give me a blessing and I didn't accept it. I was rejecting his gift. Even if I did accept the gift, could I be sure the gift was from him and that the gift was good? I'd received the gift of a second chance, the new beginning, but now I feared taking his gifts because in the time of waiting, I was out of control and did not know what was ahead.

It had been about three years since Paul's promotion to heaven, and I had made good use of the time in the waiting room as I dug deeper to discern the truth of God's word to dismantle my doubt. God's word helped me overcome fear, put aside procrastination, forgive my offenders, let go of my roles as Paul's wife, and travel courageously alone overseas.

Somehow, I knew God was going to give me the blessing of a relationship with a man, even though I was not looking for a replacement husband. I was hesitant to date or remarry, even if that was God's will for me and admitted my hesitancy. I confessed my sin of pride and my over-confidence about running my own life. I turned the reins of my life over, once again, to his capable hands. I submitted my concerns and questions to the Lord in an earnest, expectant way as I waited on what was next.

Developed by doubt

With my doubts and uncertainty, I responded to God with my emotions and with reluctance born of caution instead of handing my situation over to him in faith. Did you know that 80 percent of our problems stem from how we feel about ourselves?[3] I didn't feel I was worthy of the blessings God wanted to give me. To invite God into my "waiting room," I had to do these three things:

1. Stop. It was time once again for me to stop and pay attention to my emotions. It was essential for me to spend time alone with God and explain my feelings to him, not just aloud, but by writing them down in my journal. By doing this, I let God know I was choosing to submit to his plan. "See, I am doing a new thing! Now it springs up; do you not perceive it? I am making a way in the wilderness and streams in the wasteland" (Isaiah 43:19).
2. Confess. I told God about my fear, procrastination, and pride. I explained to him I didn't think I was worthy of

the blessings he wanted to give to me. I compared myself to other women, and those old doubts of insecurity crept in again, overshadowing everything God had shown me in the past. I had to come against and reject condemning, shaming, and blaming thoughts; by reviewing his promises, I could dig down deep into what is true. The condemning thoughts were not from him. "Therefore, there is now no condemnation for those who are in Christ Jesus" (Romans 8:1).

3. Believe. By faith, I reaffirmed my understanding that God was working behind the scenes and that no matter how long the wait or what I sensed was ahead, God's sovereignty was at work. I renewed my faith in God's providence and kept studying God's word, which brought peace and hope. "You have heard these things; look at them all. Will you not admit them? From now on I will tell you of new things, of hidden things unknown to you" (Isaiah 48:6). God asked me to wait on him and his timing.

God's waiting room

In a time of recovery, you can be sure you will spend time in God's waiting room. It helps to invite God into the waiting room with us, but we must remember that although doubt may join us there, too, we will not let it remain. When God waits with us, our faith is strengthened, our hope is renewed. We have a fresh perspective on our trials. Mary, the mother of Jesus, knew about waiting. Imagine your life interrupted by an angel who gave you news…not good news. "'Do not be afraid, Mary; you have found favor with God. You will conceive and give birth to a son, and you are to call him Jesus. He will be great and will be called the Son of the Most High'" (Luke 1:30-32). The angel left her side, and soon Mary was on her way to see her cousin, Elizabeth. At Mary's arrival, Elizabeth (the priest Zechariah's wife) was overjoyed. Luke 1:41-43 (TLB) says, "At the sound of Mary's greeting, Elizabeth's child leaped within her and she was filled with the Holy Spirit. She gave a glad cry and exclaimed to Mary, 'You are favored by God above all other women, and your child is destined for God's mightiest praise. What an honor this is, that the mother of my Lord should visit me!'"

What had happened? Elizabeth confirmed to Mary what the angel had spoken in Luke 1:30, for later Elizabeth says, "'You are blessed because you believed that the Lord would do what he said'" (Luke 1:45, NLT). How did Elizabeth know that Mary had a crisis of belief not too long before visiting her? Mary wasn't quite sure how this whole virgin birth thing could be possible. That's a pretty big crisis of belief. But Mary believed, and she gained favor with God, and somehow Elizabeth knew this. Our circumstances may not be as desperate as the unmarried, crisis pregnancy Mary experienced, but we may feel almost as distressed as she. We know Mary came to a peaceful conclusion. In Luke 1:38 we read, "'I am the Lord's servant,' Mary answered. 'May your word to me be fulfilled.'" Perhaps that is the secret to the waiting room; there can be distress, but often we are waiting for good things too. For what or on whom are you waiting?

Pay attention

When I get a small, annoying pebble inside my tennis shoe before I complete my running course, I must stop. I sit down on the curb, take off my shoe, and remove the tiny irritant. In the same way, when I least expect it, the exasperation of doubt again sneaks into my thoughts. When it does, I stop what I'm doing, sit down to figure out what is going on, and pay attention to my feelings. It takes time to examine and defeat the enemy's lies as we peel back the layers of frustration, answer questions to move forward, and reclaim peace and joy. Time in God's word helped me see and remove the irritating pebble of doubt, calm those evil thoughts, and replace them with the truth. I repeated this discipline as many times as I needed while in the waiting room with God.

I had become accustomed to my widowhood; it was becoming my identity. Someone even accused me of playing "the widow card" to get what I needed. Although I disagreed with that method and title, the comment made me consider how I acted and why. I believe that accusation was partially why I didn't think I was deserving of a new friendship with a widower. It forced me into some self-examination, and I was content with the answer. I knew my heavenly father, and gifts from him are always good. "Every good and perfect gift is from above, coming down from the Father of the heavenly lights" (James 1:17). And I knew I had acted honorably.

Waiting can be wonderful

Sometimes God's long-range plans seem blocked by a thick fog of doubt or uncertainty, and when that happens, you might feel like you are stuck in that waiting room again. No one is calling your name to move forward or get out for a long time, though others' names seem to be called. But God is a God worth waiting for. It is his plan for you to wait. Some of us might say, "I hate waiting." Me too. I can handle "No!" better than I can face "Wait." That's why our hope, our trust, our expectations must begin and end here at Isaiah 40:31: "But those who hope in the Lord will renew their strength. They will soar on wings like eagles; they will run and not grow weary, they will walk and not be faint."[4] No one likes to wait, but there are critical lessons that can be learned only from sitting on the bench. Waiting is an essential step in learning how to trust and serve God well.

If you are waiting on God, you are in good company: Joseph waited thirteen years before assuming the leadership of Egypt; Abraham waited twenty-five years before his wife Sarah gave birth to their first child; Moses waited forty years before God called him to deliver his people; David spent fourteen years before the throne of Israel would be his; Jesus waited thirty years before he began his ministry.[5] But you and I, like them, must invite God into our waiting room. He is good company.

My best gift

For years our family had been kept healthy by a gentle, godly family man who attended our church: our chiropractor, Dr. Jim Turner. I had chronic neck and back injuries that needed regular care—the result of a motorcycle accident that occurred during my teenage rebellion—so I was a weekly patient. Jim's wife, Peggy, had lost a five-year battle with breast cancer. About a year and a half after her death, he told me, "I think I am about ready to start doing things again with other singles." The comment went over my head. Right before my next week'sappointment to see him, I wondered, *Did Dr. Turner—it was odd to call him Jim—want me to do something with him?* I prayed, *God, help me to be open to your will.* That day it dawned on me, fellow-widower Jim Turner wanted to date me. I was taken aback. I wasn't sure how to respond. Boy, was I out of my comfort zone. I wasn't sure if I was ready to date. My confidence and sureness tanked as a cloud of fear and self-doubt covered the truth about God and how I felt about myself. But had this been what I'd been waiting for in God's waiting room?

Fully alive

Earlier I shared how my God-confidence led me to the comfort zone of making decisions on my own and how God was closer to me than anyone else. Elisabeth Elliot says, "Waiting on God requires the willingness to bear uncertainty, to carry within one's self the unanswered question, lifting the heart to God about it whenever it intrudes upon one's thoughts."[6] And as I consented to God's will for a relationship, and later possibly remarriage, I was confident he was asking me to trust him to do something I wouldn't have planned for myself.

I had been speaking to and teaching widows' groups around the world, from Bujumbura, Burundi, to Bakersfield, California. I read in Isaiah 54:4 (NIV), "Do not be afraid, do not fear disgrace, remember no more the disappointment of your widowhood." I looked up the meaning of disappointment; some translations say "reproach," which means displeasure, discontent. I attended church alone, went to work alone, went to support group alone. I didn't want to admit it, but I did want to remarry. But how would this work? If my status changed and I became a wife, would my ministry still be comforting to widows? God's presence in the waiting room gave me peace, no matter what he had in mind.

My best gift

We started out slowly in our relationship, but Jim Turner and I had been friends for over twenty-four years, so we knew a lot about each other. When I was diagnosed with stage IV cancer, Dr. Jim Turner was one of our key support persons, recommending chiropractic adjustments twice a week to keep my central nervous system moving; along with prayer, those sessions were essential contributors to my full recovery.

I asked God to help me trust him with my time and this new relationship. One day, the hottest day in June, Jim came over to help me clean my garage, reminiscing and chatting as we sorted and shredded files. Together we tossed out old papers and said goodbye to dead dreams, while sharing our hearts and memories of our lost loved ones. Summer days, autumn weeks, and then winter months flew by as Jim and I became good friends. We spent as much time as possible together. He invited me to take ballroom dance lessons. I invited him to go hiking, to the beach, and out of town to meet my elderly parents. We soon became inseparable; we did everything together and became each other's soul mate. We joked about our singleness. I told him I protected my heart so that I wouldn't fall in love again, and since I said I kept it in the freezer, my nickname became "the iceberg." He said when he went home from work at night, he would rather hibernate than interact with others, so his nickname became "the recluse." We got better acquainted with each other's families as it was quite evident our future would be together. This gift of a man was a blessing I wouldn't have chosen for myself. It was a gift of love I hadn't expected, but I still wondered if I was good enough for him.

Waiting on God by choice

"Waiting for God is not laziness. Waiting for God is not going to sleep. Waiting for God is not the abandonment of effort. Waiting for God means, first, activity under command; second, readiness for any new command that may come; third, the ability to do nothing until the command is given." (G. Campbell Morgan).[7] God has a plan for you and me as we wait; the wait can be a very scary process. Submitting means you and I must cooperate with him to let him change our attitude from insecurity to confidence. God-confidence.

God has our best in mind. It's really difficult to be still, to trust and to wait; that's why the waiting process must happen with God sitting near us in our waiting room. Psalm 46:10: He says, "Be still and know that I am God; I will be exalted among the nations, I will be exalted in the earth." It's in the time we stop and allow God to be God that you and I are comforted by the Holy Spirit, confident that he is working directly by our side. As we choose to work through our doubts, letting our revived faith push through, we can expect God to bring us even closer to him as we move forward into our destiny.

My Boaz has arrived

Remember the story of Ruth and Naomi? God orchestrated a redeemer to bring Ruth out of her widowed state; he provided for her and mother-in-law, Naomi. I love this story; it's so romantic, and as I was studying it during the months we dated, Jim got a new nickname to replace "the recluse." I call him "my Boaz." He has redeemed me from my widowed state, he's given me more love to share, and each day I move closer to a place of deeper healing and greater trust.

Jim and I dated for sixteen months; we were at a crossroads, in love. I kept thinking, *I just want to have fun, no strings.* And then God asked me to commit to Jim. I hadn't planned to get remarried. But my father God wanted to give me a gift, and that gift was wrapped up in the love of Jim Turner. I still loved Paul, although he had been in heaven for four years. I hadn't planned to be further healed by allowing myself to love and be loved by another man. But God had planned for that. After an invigorating hike to Yosemite Falls on Christmas Day in 2013, Jim proposed to me. I said, "Yes!" It was a beautiful setting for a brand-new beginning. We decided on a short three-month engagement, with our joyful wedding celebration to be at my home church on April 12, 2014.

On our wedding day, with peace and joy, I sat in the bride's room with my eighty-three-year-old father, who with my mother would escort me halfway down the aisle. Mom and Dad then would hand me off to my adult children, Sarah and Ben, who would escort me the remainder of the way to give me away to my groom. I received an amazing gift of love, one I didn't feel I deserved. But God did. And the good father doesn't withhold gifts from those who walk uprightly. Yes, it is true… although his blessings to me may look different from his blessings to you, good things do come to those who wait. "Not to us, Lord, not to us but to your name be the glory, because of your love and faithfulness" (Psalm 115:1).

Win by waiting

Henrietta Mears, the founder of Gospel Light Publishing, when completing her final years in ministry was asked, "If you could do anything different with your life, what would it be?" She said, "If I had my life to live over again, I would just believe God."[7] What might you do differently, starting this very day, to put your hope, all your trust in the Lord? Like Henrietta Mears, as we choose to believe God more, we can push away the clouds of doubt. Like Jesus's mother, Mary, as we present ourselves to God, submitted as his servants, we will receive the blessing of belief. Elizabeth said to Mary, "'You are blessed because you believed that the Lord would do what he said'" (Luke 1:45, NLT).

In the waiting room with God at our side, we can discern truths that others might miss; we can believe what others might doubt. Whatever it is you are waiting on, I assure you God can do it. But he might ask you to wait; I wonder, will you ask him to join you in your waiting room? I hope so.

Can you relate?

Describe a dream you have had to release.

Explain a recent interruption in your plans.

Share a crisis you have recently faced; has it moved you closer to God?

Give details about your current waiting room.

Chapter 9

THE LIGHT OF HOPE

"Hope is called the anchor of the soul, because it gives stability to the Christian life. But hope is not simply a 'wish' (I wish that such-and-such would take place); rather, it is that which latches on to the certainty of the promises of the future that God has made."
R. C. Sproul[1]

In the early morning rush hour, a crowded school bus moved tenaciously along a wet, fog-encased highway. Oklahoma state trooper Tom Taylor was working when he heard a terrible crash about twenty yards away. A jam-packed school bus, loaded with fifty-nine children, had been rear-ended by a car. Trooper Taylor didn't know what happened until he received the dispatcher's desperate call. The children on board the bus suffered mostly bumps and bruises. However, the teenage driver of the car and his friends were badly hurt and in need of urgent medical care. It was too dangerous for an ambulance to reach the scene quickly—too much fog. The dispatcher called for a med-flight helicopter to assist, but it too couldn't find the wreck.

Arriving on the scene later, Trooper George Randolf said, "The fog was so thick the med-flight couldn't see anything on the ground." The helicopter searched for several minutes before preparing to turn back, which would have left the injured passengers stranded. But Trooper Taylor—thinking quickly—remembered a small device added to the equipment in his patrol unit, a handheld GPS unit.[2]

Trooper Taylor asked if the helicopter was also equipped with a GPS and if the pilot knew how to navigate using the latitude and longitude coordinates. After Trooper Taylor was patched through to the pilot, he relayed the coordinates of his position to the med-flight helicopter. Using the coordinates, the helicopter pilot hovered above the accident scene and then slowly descended toward it. "As it got close to the ground," said Randolph, "the helicopter itself actually pushed the fog away, so the pilot could see to land and complete the rescue."

Spiritually, you and I can use the same approach; we have the right safety equipment: the GPS is our faith in Christ. The coordinates? The latitude is God's word, and the longitude is his character. When we "land" near our calamity, the power of the Holy Spirit's deafening wind blows the fog of our doubt away. We are "rescued" by the strengthening of our faith: our liberation is complete, our hope renewed, our belief restored. As I've learned to trust God more deeply, my roots of trust have grown stronger as I've stayed centered on the word of God and relied on God's faithfulness. Worry, fear, and doubt were no longer a threat to my daily joy because my doubt was converted into belief. I hope you've experienced the same victory.

All hope is ours

In the preceding chapter, we discussed the good gifts God gave me by giving me a new husband. But wait, there's more! Yes, that's right; there are more good gifts our heavenly father wants to give all of us. God's gift to us is hope. The Webster dictionary defines hope as "expectation of something we desire; a thing that gives, or an object of focus." Hebrews 6:19 defines hope this way: "We have this hope as an anchor for the soul, firm and secure."

The Bible assures us there is such a thing as real hope, and this light of hope dispels the darkness of our doubt. Hebrews 11:1 continues, "Now faith is confidence in what we hope for and assurance about what we do not see." Romans 8:24 adds, "But hope that is seen is no hope at all." When we put these two verses together, we see that hope refers to the promises of God, even when the fulfillment of these promises is still in the future and unseen. When we hope in God, we fix our eyes on his promises rather than on nagging doubt or unwanted circumstances. As believers, a Christ-centered hope must be the foundation of our lives. It is this light of Christ in us that shines to a world that desperately needs to know he can bring the very same hope to their lives.

Twenty-three million Americans suffer from anxiety disorders, another 17.5 million struggle with clinical depression, and 530,000 attempt suicide each year. Others endure daily feelings of fear and hopelessness. Airline passengers worry about flight safety, while patients agonize over the dangers of surgery or seriousness of their conditions. Business people fret because of corporate decisions, and collegians shudder at the uncertain future of their careers. A shocking 62 percent of Christians in America are worried about the future and another 20 percent are searching for meaning and purpose in life.[3] What would happen if these precious ones began to doubt their doubts? Can you imagine the revival that might take place if both nonbelievers and believers went boldly to God and asked him to prove his love? What if Christians vulnerably shared their doubts with God and invited their friends to help them doubt their doubts to strengthen their faith? Sometimes faith comes in an instant, sometimes it takes years, and sometimes faith is lost and only found again many years later. Faith can be a process, but when mixed with hope, it is sure to bring the light.

Faith-doubt=hope

Hope is much more than mere wishful thinking. Let's consider the opposite of hope—hopelessness—which ushers in doubt and brings on despair, depression, and even thoughts of suicide. Proverbs 13:12 reminds us, "Hope deferred makes the heart sick." No wonder the Bible approaches hopelessness differently from guilt, anxiety, and even depression. Instead of categorizing hopelessness—also known as despair—as a psychological disease, the Bible calls it disobedience. It is refusing to trust God, which is unbelief. Hebrews 3:12–13 shares, "See to it, brothers and sisters, that none of you has a sinful, unbelieving heart that turns away from the living God. But encourage one another daily, as long as it is called 'Today,' so that none of you may be hardened by sin's deceitfulness." We can trust the pages of history to confirm this truth in the wisdom of one of our faith fathers.

John Calvin, known as one of the fathers of Protestantism, believed Christians should not fear doubt but should expect it and not be surprised when it comes. He reminds us, "For unbelief is so deeply rooted in our hearts, and we are so inclined to it, that not without hard struggle is each one able to persuade himself of what all confess with the mouth: namely, that God is faithful."[4] Doubt is an important part of the faith experience, because in our frail human nature, we find ideas about God and his goodness so outside of our own experience that they are difficult, at first, to comprehend.

When we ask God to replace our doubt, dread, and discouragement with hope, our trust in his faithfulness is revived. Why would we hope in medication, therapy, or anything else before we hope in God? Joyce Meyer says, "Hope is favorable and confident expectation, an expectant attitude that something good is going to happen and things will work out no matter what we are facing."[5] Because of our position in Christ, our identity in Christ, all hope is ours. We can ask for a new downpour of revitalizing, refreshing hope to cleanse us from the fog of doubt as we claim the promises in his word: "May the God of hope fill you with all joy and peace as you trust in him, so that you may overflow with hope by the power of the Holy Spirit" (Romans 15:13).

New beginning

On our wedding day, Jim and I joined hands, hearts, and households. Literally. After the wedding we began blending our lives, and most important, our families and our ministries. Jim continued practicing chiropractic as he had for forty years, and he was content and productive in his work, making sick people well. On the other hand, the hours of my workday responsibilities were adjusted by my supervisor because of changes in my marital status. Things felt uneasy.

I recognized the familiar, irritating feeling when the pesky intruder, doubt, came knocking at the back door of my faith. Would I let it in? This time I understood that its intent was to dismantle my faith. And so, I sent doubt away. I was able to do this when I honestly shared my thoughts with God; what set me free was to tell God exactly how I felt. I knew God had become part of the process of my belief. I told God I didn't understand the staff and ministry changes in both organizations in which I worked. The roles I held changed, and I was free to do what was next instead of holding a job to support myself. What God had in store for my ministries now that I had remarried was yet to be revealed, but I felt like I had permission to do it. I understood that I wouldn't have 100 percent perfect faith all the time, yet I was confident about God's provision and anticipated God's goodness.

This time I knew what to do; I gave myself space and time to process my beliefs as I remembered the steps.

1. Admit my doubts. Make a list, describe the details of the specific doubt I face, and in prayer ask God to help me find his truth. This is the tension of doubt and belief; when we give God the opportunity, he wants to grow our faith. We can seek out promises to guard our hearts and minds against future doubts. "Do not be anxious about anything, but in every situation, by prayer and petition, with thanksgiving, present your requests to God. And the peace of God, which transcends all understanding, will guard your hearts and your minds in Christ Jesus" (Philippians 4:6-7).

2. Renew my mind. Our doubts come from how we feel, not what we know. We must remind ourselves what is true from God's word. Faith is the opposite of doubt; to rid ourselves of emotional or intellectual doubt is to replace our doubt with the truth. "Sanctify them by the truth; your word is truth" (John 17:17).

3. Repeat as often as needed: Admit, Renew, Repeat. We must hit repeat, rewind, replay as often as is needed, even in those times when all is well and especially when we are overwhelmed. It's a good practice to take God's word in even when we do not doubt so that the word will be available to us when we do! John 20:29 says, "Then Jesus told him [Thomas], 'Because you have seen me, you have believed; blessed are those who have not seen and yet have believed.'"

Let's look to the example of a notable Bible figure to see what he did about his doubt, or maybe what he should have done.

John the doubter

The messenger God sent to prepare the way for the coming of Jesus Christ was a wild-looking man who had no power in the Jewish political system. Yet Jesus said John the baptist was greater than any man ever born of a woman, men that include Abraham, Joseph, Moses, and David. "'Truly I tell you, among those born of women there has not risen anyone greater than John the Baptist'" (Matthew 11:11). However, John doubted the most important thing. He questioned whether Jesus was the Christ.

John's entire lifespan of thirty years was spent preparing the way for Jesus, and his ministry lasted only six months. John, like you and I, spent time in the "waiting room" with God by his side growing into a man of faith. And look at the far-reaching effect of his ministry! What an example for us. How will you spend your time in the waiting room? Will you be worried, fearful, or doubtful? Or will you be hopeful, faithful, and prayerful? We have a choice to invite God into our waiting room, and when we do so, our faith changes how we wait. It also changes how those who are waiting for us outside the waiting room respond.

Thousands of people from various nations heard John teach and prophesy. Matthew 3:1-3 says "In those days John the Baptist came, preaching in the wilderness of Judea and saying, 'Repent, for the kingdom of heaven has come near.' This is he who was spoken of through the prophet Isaiah: "A voice of one calling in the wilderness, 'Prepare the way for the Lord, make straight paths for him.'"

God showed John who Jesus was through a visible sign, as we read in Luke 3:21-22: "When all the people were being baptized, Jesus was baptized too. And as he was praying, heaven was opened and the Holy Spirit descended on him in bodily form like a dove. And a voice came from heaven: 'You are my Son, whom I love; with you I am well pleased.'" At that time John was vehemently certain Jesus was the Christ. He had zero doubt: "'I have seen and I testify that this is God's Chosen One'" (John 1:34).

However, after John was locked up in prison, he began to doubt. This tells us a most important fact: anyone, even the great John the Baptist, can be a victim of doubt. Jesus responded wonderfully. He told the disciples to go to visit John in prison and to share with him the miracles they'd seen. Jesus promised that John would be blessed if he would only believe. Matthew 11:4-6 tells us, "Jesus replied, 'Go back and report to John what you hear and see: The blind receive sight, the lame walk, those who have leprosy are cleansed, the deaf hear, the dead are raised, and the good news is proclaimed to the poor. Blessed is anyone who does not stumble on account of me.'"

Jesus reminded John of the scriptures, which is exactly what he wants to remind us of too. His desire is for us to go to the word of God and discover penetrating truth to bring the light of hope into our situations. When we do, we overcome our doubt. You can be sure we will always face situations when we feel fogged in; let's not wait too long to turn on the light.

The light of hope

Just as a ship makes a fresh path through an uncharted sea, I navigated new territory. I'd moved past my previous life; feeling the warmth of renewed optimism, I left my job situations behind. I no longer needed the grief support group or my weekly counseling appointments, yet I jealously guarded my daily time alone with God. If I fulfilled my commitment to him by showing up, he was already there, waiting for our time of loving fellowship. His word continued to give me daily guidance as I put in the time for daily prayer, praise, and study. "The precepts of the Lord are right, giving joy to the heart. The commands of the Lord are radiant, giving light to the eyes" (Psalm 19:8). I hope you take time daily to turn on the light.

In our new life together, not only did Jim and I unite our hands and hearts but also we brought together our six children, each married. At the time of our glorious wedding, most of our children had their own children. Our grandchildren, precious and impressionable, enlarged our hearts to an even greater capacity. As newlyweds, setting up house was a bunch of fun and work; we enjoyed mixing the furniture and appliances of our former lives into one new whole. Now it was time for our children and us to blend our hearts into one new family by getting to know each other better. We committed early on to support each other's memories of our deceased spouses, who were our children's parents, by finding ways to honor them. We instilled traditions for the holidays, their birthdays, and "death-iversaries," and gave extra time when our children needed special comfort as they missed their deceased parent. During this season, I found myself in the "waiting room" again, as I invited God into the process of blending our lives. I wanted to hurry through it; God encouraged me to "be still" as I waited.

As the new spouse of a former widower, at times I've felt I must be a sorry replacement, second-best, fill-in, and sometimes unwanted stepmother. Lies, deceit, and doubt. I knew what to do: Admit, Renew, Repeat. I challenged these pesky thoughts, the dark ones clouding the view of my world and my contributions to the family. I sent them away, straight out into the light as I turned to God's word. I was reminded of my role in the family and God's kingdom through Isaiah 61:1: "The Spirit of the Sovereign LORD is on me, because the LORD has anointed me to proclaim good news to the poor. He has sent me to bind up the brokenhearted." I knew that once again I must let go of my plans and expectations to let God work through me. God renewed my hope through his word and my obedience to pray for myself, my new husband, our children, and our grandchildren. This could happen only if I maintained a deep prayer life.

I don't want to be lost in the fog, wandering in the dark or blinded by a little doubt. With confidence, I remind myself, "The Lord is my light and my salvation—whom shall I fear? The Lord is the stronghold of my life—of whom shall I be afraid?" (Psalm 27:1).

Happy ending

I've found the sure way to overcome doubt is to get to the place where God's word is real and alive. It should be more genuine than anything you or I can see, taste, hear, smell, or feel. When you and I are in doubt, we can refer to the word of God in the same way Jesus told John the Baptist to do. "Consequently, faith comes from hearing the message, and the message is heard through the word about Christ" (Romans 10:17).

We know God answers heartfelt prayers that cry, "Help my unbelief." When doubts threaten to upend our faith, the tiny seed of faith in that prayer is more than enough to not only help us survive but also restore our hope and blow away the fog of doubt. I learned that no matter what comes my way, what doubts I offer up, it'll be okay. God makes it so.

Can you relate?

Share how your hope has been renewed.

Describe the difference between doubt and belief.

Discuss how your faith has been strengthened as the truth has overcome your doubt.

Express one or two truths you have learned because of reading this book.

Do you trust now that it'll be okay?

LOVE LETTER TO MY READERS

Dear Readers, because we are building upon a premise of God's love, I want to make sure you have a foundation laid as you navigate from doubt to belief. I can't wait to share with you a truth that can change your life. God sent His only son, Jesus Christ, to die in our place. He would have done this if you, or I, were the only person on earth. That's how much God loves us. God's love is unconditional; God's love is perfect. How do we know God loves us? His word tells us.

"But God demonstrates His own love for us in this: While we were still sinners, Christ died for us" (Romans 5:8). God created us in his image—for a relationship with him—but he gave us freedom of choice. We could choose to partake in a love relationship with him or not. Because of our sin, we are separated from a holy God. Romans 3:23 tells us, "For all have sinned and fall short of the glory of God." In Romans 6:23 we learn, "For the wages of sin is death, but the gift of God is eternal life in Christ Jesus our Lord." There is only one penalty for the sin that separates us from God - death. Some try to earn their way to heaven by working hard or being religious, but Hebrews 9:22 says, "Without the shedding of blood, there is no forgiveness." Jesus Christ is the only answer to the problem. He died on the cross and rose from the grave, paying the "death penalty" for our sin. He provided a way for us to have a relationship with God.

As you read through John 3:16 aloud, fill your name in the blanks. "For God so loved _____ that he gave his one and only Son, that if _____believes in him, _____ shall not perish but have eternal life." What an amazing love. God sent his son, his only son, Jesus, to die for us. Which one of us would give our children—our only child—for the lives of someone else? God did, for you. Imagine God making way for a relationship with him by giving his only son as a sacrifice. You, however, must make a choice. You must choose to accept and believe.

Are you separated from God? I want you to be totally honest with God. Is there any reason why you cannot receive Jesus right now? God has loved you since before the beginning of time. He gave you a gift. His son Jesus Christ died for you on the cross and rose from the grave. Jesus cares for you, and he calls you to decide for him today. He has a plan for your life. Don't miss out on the life God has for you. We can't clean up our act ourselves. I know. I've tried. We can't work our way to a relationship with God, and we can't get there by being religious. God has allowed Jesus's blood to cover our sins so that we can have fellowship with him. In 1 John 1:9 we read, "If we confess our sins, he is faithful and just and will forgive us our sins and purify us from all unrighteousness."

God is asking you to give yourself totally and completely to him. Jesus had victory over death when he rose from the dead. Literally, Jesus Christ took on our sin; he was our substitute so that we might become the righteousness of God. When God sees us, he doesn't see our sin—he sees us through Jesus Christ. Because of Jesus Christ's finished work on the cross, we have access to live life through his power. In Christ, we are new creatures. 2 Corinthians 5:17 says, "Therefore, if anyone is in Christ, the new creation has come: The old has gone, the new is here!"

Pray this prayer to invite Jesus Christ to come in and control your life through the Holy Spirit. If you have already received Christ at one time in your life but feel you would like to recommit your life and your family to Christ, you can pray this prayer too.

Dear Lord Jesus, I know that I am a sinner and need your forgiveness. I believe that you died for my sins. I want to turn from my sins. I now invite you to come into my heart and life. I want to trust and follow you as Lord and Savior. In Jesus's name, amen.

God loves you, and so do I.

Sheryl

ENDNOTES

Chapter 1: Pat Answers

1. http://time.com/4126238/mother-teresas-crisis-of-faith/ (12/11/2017)
2. http://www.commdiginews.com/life/studies-reflect-the-damage-of-the-one-parent-fatherless-family-17573/ (9/15/2016)
3. http://www.commdiginews.com/life/studies-reflect-the-damage-of-the-one-parent-fatherless-family-17573/ (9/15/2016)
4. C. S. Lewis, Mere Christianity (New York, NY: Harper-Collins, 1952), 25
5. http://www.christinyou.net/pages/doubt.html (11/10/2017)
6. John Ortberg. AZQuotes.com, Wind and Fly LTD, 2017 (12/26/2017)

7. Alfred, Lord Tennyson, https://www.brainyquote.com/quotes/alfred_lord_tennyson_161107 (12/27/2017)

8. Frederick Buechner, Secrets in the Dark (HarperCollins, 2007)

Chapter 2: Did God Hear?

1. www.dailymail.co.uk/woman-living-water-stops-day-47 (10/1/2017)

2. Brennan Manning, Abba's Child, (Colorado Springs, CO: Navpress, 2002), 35

3. Neil T. Anderson & Steve Goss, Freedom In Christ (Oxford, UK & Grand Rapids, MI: Monarch Books, 2004, 2009), 132

4. Neil T. Anderson & Steve Goss, Freedom In Christ (Oxford, UK & Grand Rapids, MI: Monarch Books, 2004, 2009), 133

5. https://psychology1.knoji.com/therapy-is-like-peeling-an-onion/ (12/4/2017)

6. Neil T. Anderson, Victory Over The Darkness (Ventura, CA: Regal Books/Gospel Light, 1990, 2000), 25

7. http://ficm.org/about-us/#!/who-i-am-in-christ (12/4/2017)

8. Upon author's written permission, use of Who I Am In Christ granted by Baker Publishing Group, January 10, 2018

Chapter 3: Now What?

1. http://www.azquotes.com/author/17661-Os_Guinness (9/15/2017)

2. https://www.farmersalmanac.com/weather/2015/03/16/5-foggiest-places-north-america/ (11/25/2017)

3. David Jeremiah, A Bend In The Road, W Publishing Group - Thomas Nelson, 21

4. https://lovegodgreatly.com/week-1-naomi-loss/ (12/7/2017)

5. Life Application Study Bible: New Living Translation (2004) John Profiles - Thomas - John 20:27-28

6. David Jeremiah, A Bend In The Road, W Publishing Group - Thomas Nelson, 21

7. Rick Warren, The Purpose Driven Life, (Grand Rapids, Michigan) Zondervan, 2002, 107

Chapter 4: Not Sure

1. https://relevantmagazine.com/god/7-prominent-christian-thinkers-who-wrestled-doubt (12/11/2017)

2. https://www.blueletterbible.org/lang.lexicon.cfm?Strongs=H8615&t=KJV (1/4/2018)

3. Jerry Bridges, The Beauty of Holiness (Colorado Springs, CO: Navigators/NavPress, 1989), 34

4. Neil T. Anderson, Victory Over The Darkness (Ventura, CA: Regal Books/Gospel Light, 1990, 2000), 25

5. H. Norman Wright, Experiencing Grief (Nashville, TN:B & H Publishing Group, 2004), 19

6. GriefShare is a ministry of Church Initiative, Wake Forest, NC. To find a group near you or to start a group: www.griefshare.org, info@griefshare.org, 800-395-5755

Chapter 5: I'm Afraid

1. https://philmgreen.wordpress.com/2010/09/13/idoubt-1-thirteen-quotes-about-doubt/ (10/10/2017)
2. https://christianpost.com/news/ministry-joyce-meyer-defeat-doubt-unbelief-faith-god-bible-abraham-154066/MakeUpYourMindtoBelieve (11/20/2017)
3. https://www.georgemueller.org/quotes/category/faith (9/10/201)
4. H. Norman Wright, Experiencing Grief (Nashville, TN:B & H Publishing Group, 2004), 3, 4
5. Neil Anderson & Steve Goss, Freedom In Christ Discipleship Course (Monarch Books, UK), 171

Chapter 6: This Too Shall Pass

1. https://philmgreen.wordpress.com/2010/09/13/idoubt-1-thirteen-quotes-about-doubt/ (11/1/2017)
2. http://www.beliefnet.com/faiths/galleries/5-famous-christians-who-struggled-with-doubt.aspx?p=3(12/1/2017)
3. https://www.bibletools.org/index.cfm/fuseaction/Lexicon.show/ID/H6342/pachad. (9/10/2013)
4. https://www.merriam-webster.com/dictionary/procrastinate (12/15/2017)
5. Priscilla Shirer, Jonah: Navigating a Life Interrupted (Lifeway Press, Nashville, TN) 2010, 37
6. Neil T. Anderson, The Steps to Freedom In Christ, Gospel Light, (Ventura, CA, 2004), 12
7. Neil T. Anderson, The Steps to Freedom In Christ, Gospel Light, (Ventura, CA, 2004), 12

8. https://relevantmagazine.com/god/7-prominent-christian-thinkers-who-wrestled-doubt (12/1/2017)

Chapter 7: Second Chance
1. https://www.deseretnews.com/top/817/0/Top-100-CS-Lewis-quotes-.html (1/6/2018)
2. https://www.nps.gov/yell/learn/nature/1988fires.htm (1/10/2015)
3. https://rachelheldevans.com/blog/christian-survival-guide-doubt-ed-cyzewski (11/15/2017)
4. http://latindiscussion.com/forum/latin/capax-dei.1065/ (10/15/2016)
5. https://www.goodreads.com/quotes/920790-when-it-comes-to-god-we-can-t-run-out-of (1/10/2018)

Chapter 8: You'll Be Fine
1. https://www.goodreads.com/work/quotes/239588-waiting-on-god (1/2/2018)
2. https://www.michealhyatt.com/what-to-do-while-you-are-waiting (1/5/2018)
3. http://www.joycemeyer.com/how-to-defeat-your-doubts-and-feed-your-faith/ (11/15/2017)
4. http://www.lizcurtishiggs.com/the-20-verses-you-love-most-10-flying-high/ (10/15/2016)
5. http://christianfunnypictures.com/2015/03/joesph-waited-13-years-abraham-waited.html (10/15/2017)
6. https://www.goodreads.com/author/quotes/6264.Elisabeth_Elliot (9/1/2017)

7. https://www.goodreads.com/quotes/333742-waiting-for-god-is-not-laziness-waiting-for-god-is (9-1-2017)

8. http://www.azquotes.com/author/20430-Henrietta_Mears/(1/10/2017)

Chapter 9: The Light of Hope

1. https://www.crosswalk.com/faith/spiritual-life/inspiring-quotes/25-quotes-to-give-you-hope.html (1/8/2018)

2. http://www.govtech.com/magazines/gt/Rescue-In-The-Fog.html (1/10/2018)

3. http:// www.expositor.org/nov-dec-03.sw (2/15/2016)

4. https://www.biblestudytools.com/history/calvin-institutes-christianity/book3/chapter-2.htm (1/3/2018)

5. https://www.brainyquote.com/quotes/joyce_meyer_567618 (10/10/2016)

DEDICATION

I dedicate this book to my husband, Dr. Jim Turner. Jim, my Boaz, you are loving, encouraging, prayerful, and persistent. I am amazed by your belief in me and thankful for the burden we share to help the hurting. Sweetheart, I am honored to be your wife, and I'll love you forever.

"If you believe, you will receive whatever you ask for in prayer." Matthew 21:22

"'If you can'?" said Jesus. "Everything is possible for one who believes." Mark 9:23

ACKNOWLEDGMENTS

To my husband, our children, and grandchildren: Each of you is a gift from God. Because of you, my life is richer, and I've discovered new depths of love I never imagined. I love you all.

To the board members, prayer partners, and financial supporters of From Ashes to Beauty, Inc.: Thank you for standing with Jim and me. We are grateful for your loyalty and true friendship as we journey in reaching out to the nations with the love of Jesus Christ.

To Athena, Sandra, and Kate: Thank you for your diligence in publishing and polishing this message and for your business expertise and editing skills. I am in awe of your God-given gifts and our God-ordained partnership.

To Amber: Thank you for a spectacular cover design for this message. It's engaging and informative, inviting readers to find within the pages how to move from doubt to a deeper faith.

To Carol, Jim, and Sandra: Thank you for reading this message in its formative stages and giving wise input on difficult decisions.

To our Father, our Lord Jesus Christ, and the Holy Spirit: Thank you for saving us completely from our sins, adopting us as your children, and entrusting us with the message of hope and healing for your beloved people. You deserve all the glory, honor, and praise.

> *Then Jesus said to the centurion, "Go! Let it be done just as you believed it would."*
> *And his servant was healed at that moment. Matthew 8:13*

AUTHOR INFORMATION

Exchanging hurt for hope is Sheryl Giesbrecht Turner's focus—a message she shares with audiences as a radio and television personality, compelling author, and sought-after speaker. A dynamic teacher and motivating leader, Giesbrecht Turner has endured many changes and challenges, moving her to a deep faith in and reliance upon God.

She served as Focus on the Family's columnist for Pastor's Wives for four years. Hundreds of her columns and magazine and devotional articles have appeared in various publiscations, including *Focus on The Family Magazine, Just Between Us, Discipleship Journal, CCM, Walk Thru the Bible's - InDeed* and *Tapestry, Charisma, Faith Filled Family, iBelieve, Live Living, Spirit-Led Woman.* She is a monthly contributor to the Lead Like Jesus blogspot.

Giesbrecht Turner's television and radio show, "Transformed Through Truth," is nationally and internationally syndicated, viewed and heard daily by audiences of over 20 million on audio, internet, Roku, and YouTube networks across the United States and on seven continents with The Holy Spirit Broadcasting Network www.HSBN.tv.

Sheryl is passionate about reaching out to the poor and needy, locally through The Mission at Kern County and worldwide through various international ministry partners. Giesbrecht Turner is a Lead Like Jesus Facilitator and monthly blogger at www.leadlikejesus.com as well as a missionary with Freedom In Christ Ministries www.FICM.org. She has been personally involved with equipping hundreds for ministry and facilitating the training of thousands of leaders internationally.

The joys of Giesbrecht Turner's life are her children and thirteen grandchildren. She is excited about the newest chapter in her life, her recent marriage to Dr. Jim Turner. Sheryl holds a bachelor of arts from Biola University, a master's in ministry, and a doctorate of theology.

Sign up to receive Sheryl's weekly blog on her website:
www.fromashestobeauty.com.

Follow Sheryl on her Facebook pages:
Sheryl Giesbrecht Turner and *@AuthorSherylGiesbrecht*

Twitter:
@SGiesbrecht

Instagram:
sherylgiesbrecht.

ORDER INFORMATION

REDEMPTION PRESS

To order additional copies of this book, please visit
www.redemption-press.com.
Also available on Amazon.com and BarnesandNoble.com
Or by calling toll free 1-844-2REDEEM.